New England's Bounty

Katie Moose

Conduit Press
Annapolis, MD

Front cover design: Jean Harper Baer, Baltimore, Maryland

Copyright ©2004   Conduit Press

Published by Conduit Press, 111 Conduit Street, Annapolis, Maryland 21401.

Library of Congress Cataloging-in-Publication Data

Printed and Bound by United Book Press, Inc. Baltimore, Maryland, USA

ISBN: 0-9666610-8-7

TABLE OF CONTENTS

PICTURES

INTRODUCTION

The author's mother and father, Mr. and Mrs. William Hadwen Barney at their wedding reception at the Women's City Club, Boston on September 25, 1944. They were married at Christ Church, the oldest church in Cambridge, built in 1761 and designed by Peter Harrison of Newport. They spent their honeymoon on Nantucket at the Barnacle, our family home on Swain's Wharf.

"We'll drink a glass in Barney's Bar
To you, good ship, so there you are,
A Merchant Ship, a Liberty,
Another tramp upon the sea."
Anonymous

New England blood has been in my blood from both sides of my family and dates back to the original settlers. My parents met on Nantucket on August 12, 1944 and my father proposed on August 13th. My mother and father are sixth cousins, descendants of the Starbucks.

Almost every summer since I was a little girl we'd spend summers on Nantucket, although one vacation my parents rented a house in Chatham. That was the first time I learned about sharks when Dad and Uncle Ches Baum caught a small one. But most of our fishing days were spent catching blue fish, still a summer favorite. Looking for mussels or clams for Sunday dinner along the Jetty is now a long ago memory. There may still be some there, but alas we're not allowed to walk out on the rocks anymore. Even better was to go to the local seafood market for lobster. My grandmothers cooked up a feast – lobster, corn on the cob, lots of melted butter, and finally when we'd made a real mess, the finger bowls and towels were brought out to clean up. Dining was a formal affair, seated in the dining room with the best linens and silver, even though this was summer vacation. Dinner promptly at 1 on Sundays and you had better be dressed in your Sunday best.

Over the years I traveled extensively throughout New England, often visiting family and friends. My daughter and I lived in Newport and Providence, and later I spent time in Greenwich. We'd ski, sail, go to the beach everywhere from Stowe to Westport Harbor or back to our beloved Nantucket. At my daughter's school each senior had to give a ten minute talk. Lucinda reminisced about Nantucket and fond memories of her great grandmothers. Now its time spent with her grandparents.

New England is beautiful anytime of the year. But it is the bounty of the land that keeps bringing us back. The delicious fruits and vegetables of the summer and fall, maple syrup, ice cream cones on a hot day, or Indian pudding or blueberries for dessert.

New England's Bounty is my fourth cookbook. The recipes either come from the family, friends, or those developed here at home. Each book contains a history chapter and recipes that are easy to fix, but elegant. So enjoy the bounty of New England.

HISTORICAL FACTS ON NEW ENGLAND

Joseph Starbuck Barney of Nantucket, the author's great grandfather

Beginning about 2500 BC tribes of the Algonquin language group inhabited New England. Norsemen were the first Europeans to explore the region and may have gotten as far south as Rhode Island. From 1450-1500 Basque fishermen explored the fishing grounds off New England.

Cape Cod was named in 1602 by Bartholomew Gosnold for "the great store of cod-fish" that he found while exploring the region. Gosnold and John Brereton, English explorers, also landed on Martha's Vineyard in 1602. Brereton wrote of "the incredible store of vines and the beautie and delicacie of this sweet soil". The island was named for Mr Gosnold's daughter, Martha.

John Smith explored Boston Harbor and Piscataqua in 1614. He found the islands were inhabited and "were planted with corn, groves, mulberries, savage gardens". Also in 1614 Adriaen Block a Dutchman, explored the Connecticut River as far as Enfield Falls.

The Native Americans, the Wampanoags farmed, fished, gathered wild fruits and berries, and caught whales. The Native Americans planted their crops in the spring near their villages, and often moved along streams or nearer to the sea to collect seafood and shells, and would return to the villages for their fall harvest and hunting game, including turkey. The Pilgrims made landfall first at Provincetown in 1620 and arriving in Plymouth, found a harsh land, but with a good, protected harbor and fresh water. The Wampanoags taught the Pilgrims how to till the land, such as putting fish in each corn hill for fertilizer, and how to catch the fish and game supply. Some of their vegetables-corn and squash, hominy, corn pone, and succotash; wild leeks, onions, beans and acorns saved the first settlers. There was an abundance of seafood – mussels, clams, lobsters and fish.

The observance of the first Thanksgiving occurred with the harvest of the first crop in 1621. Thirty-five more Pilgrims arrived that year and found other staples such as soft-shell crabs, beach plums, groundnuts, and berries to sustain them. They planted maize, wheat, barley and peas, but all fail except the maize. By 1622 the harvest was almost non-existent, but pumpkins ease the food shortage. However, by 1625 the colony managed to have a sufficient supply. Pilgrims in the Massachusetts Bay Colony resorted to eating passenger pigeons in 1643 to survive. By 1736 passenger pigeons were selling at six for a penny in Boston. In 1749 all of New England suffered a severe drought.

The Casco Bay Peninsula in Maine was settled by the French and English beginning in 1623. Other settlers arrived from Massachusetts in 1715, and by 1770 Falmouth received its name. The colonists' livelihoods included fishing, furs, lumber and masts for the British Navy. On July 4, 1786 Falmouth was renamed Portland. Shipbuilding was to become a major industry. In 1885 the Portland Sugar Company became one of the first refineries in the United States.

Gloucester, Massachusetts, founded in 1623 by Pilgrim immigrants, is the oldest fishing port still in continuous operation. The world's first two-masted schooner was launched here in 1713 to fish the Grand Banks and Newfoundland, further off the coast than the Stellwagen Bank, whose catch was being depleted even in those early years of large catches. Gloucester Adventure, a non-profit organization has restored the *Adventure*, the last American dory fishing trawler, which was built in Essex in 1926 and caught over $4 million in cod and halibut. The restoration is located in Fitz Hugh Lane Park, named for Gloucester's famous marine painter. Growing up, one of the author's favorite movies was *Captains Courageous,* a story by Rudyard Kipling about Gloucester.

Nearby Rockport was also a fishing village until after the Civil War when it became an artist's colony. Essex once had at least fifteen shipyards producing over 50 boats a year, including fishing schooners. Shipyards at Newburyport produced 107 ships between 1681 and 1741.

Quincy, MA famous as the "City of Presidents" was founded in 1624. In 1625 Thomas Morton, one of the original settlers, traded liquor and firearms to the Native Americans, infuriating the Pilgrims. He was arrested by Myles Standish, and sent back to England

Salem, MA was settled in 1626 by Roger Conant and a group of fishermen that came over from Cape Ann. The harbor was protected, and the town grew prosperous through fishing and trade with England, France, Spain, the Netherlands and the West Indies, and eventually to Asia for spices, silks, coffee and tea. The Derby Wharf is named for Elias Derby, a successful merchant, and America's first millionaire and a runner of privateers during the Revolution. The Warehouse displays items brought on board the ships such as tea chests. The Hawthorne House, built in 1682 is known as "the old bakery". One of the most incredible collections of American and Asian items is found at the Peabody Museum, the oldest continuously operating museum in the United States, founded by sea captains in 1799 as the East India Marine Society. Treasures include magnificent tea services, silver, furniture, maritime instruments, and ship models. The double service of Canton export porcelain, purchased by Sally Ropes and Joseph Orne for their wedding in 1817 at the Ropes Museum is also noteworthy. The Lindall-Gibbs-Osgood House was the boyhood home of Benjamin Thompson, later Count Rumford, who invented the Rumford stove, oven and fireplace. The Pioneer Village, built in 1930 for the 300th anniversary of the arrival of the *Arbella*, which brought Governor John Winthrop to Salem, and recreates Roger Conant's settlement. Basins collected sea water that was evaporated to extract salt for curing food.

Sandwich, MA, founded in 1627, served as a farming and whaling community. The Boston & Sandwich Glass Company, founded in 1825, produced large numbers of glass items for the home. Today the Sandwich Glass Museum displays many of these treasures.

Marblehead, MA, settled as a plantation of Salem in 1629 by fishermen from Cornwall and the Channel Islands, thrived from fishing, especially codfish which was laid out to dry, shipbuilding; and trading. In 1774 when the governor closed the port of Boston, Marblehead allowed Boston merchants to land here.

Portsmouth, NH, settled in 1631, was named Piscataqua by the governor of the Plymouth Colony. Later it was known Strawbery Banke, named for the strawberries nearby, and in 1653 incorporated as Portsmouth. The islands off here were used to dry cod. Portsmouth also made its livelihood from farming and shipbuilding. The Inn at Strawbery Banke dates to 1800 and is part of the Strawbery Banke Museum. Next door to this is the 18th Oracle House Inn, which was the home of an officer in the British Navy. *The Oracle*, the first newspaper in New Hampshire, was published here. Dunfey's Restaurant is on board the MV John Wanamaker, the last active steam tug in U.S. coastal waters.

The Dutch built a fort and trading post at Hartford, CT in 1633, leaving in 1654. The English had started settling into the region in 1635, led by John Steele. Trade included furs, timber, fish and tobacco, which is still grown in the state. Hartford and Wethersfield prospered as shipping ports. Wethersfield, as early as the 1640s, was exporting barrel staves, fish, salt beef, corn and pork. Warehouses dating from 1690 are still along the river. After 1700 the town expanded into lumber, beaver skins, bricks and onions. In return molasses, rum, sugar and wool were imported. Later the river was to change its course and the port moved to Rocky Hill. The Cove Warehouse is the U.S. only remaining warehouse from the 17th c.

Berlin, CT was founded by Edward and William Pattison in 1740, who produced the first tin ware in the United States which was sold door-to-door. Tin ware was also manufactured in Southington with machinery patented by Seth Peck.

The Connecticut River valley provided good farmland, but also an abundance of trees that were used for barrels to transport rum and molasses as part of the Triangular Trade. Cattle, horses, pigs, wheat and coffee were also raised here. Silk was grown in central Connecticut. The northwestern part of Connecticut contained iron ore deposits. The ore was smelted and made into nails, cooking utensils and other implements beginning in the 1730s. The farmers and iron mongers were a major provider of food and arms to the Continental Army during the Revolution. Connecticut came to be known as the "Provisions State".

Essex was also an important trading and shipbuilding center with eight shipyards. Rum, molasses, sugar and ivory for piano keys were imported. Essex was a commercial stop on the Connecticut River for steamboats. New Haven too made its name as a port, importing tea, silk and porcelains from China. The city also traded with the eastern coastal towns and the West Indies. Branford was founded in 1638 when the New Haven colony purchased land from the Native Americans. A saltworks provided salt to preserve food during the Revolutionary War.

Derby, CT, founded during the 1640s as a trading post, was later a trading port for shipping lumber, livestock and foodstuff in exchange for rum, wine, fruit, brandy and slaves.

Stonington, CT, once a fishing village, today has Connecticut's largest commercial fishing fleet. Mystic Seaport known for its whaling ships, including the Charles W. Morgan the last wooden whaling ship, also displays the L.A. Dunton, a 1921 fishing schooner and the last example of the round-bow fishing vessel used in New England to splat and salt cod.

Guilford, once a farming community, later had mills and a shipyard. Fish were transported to New York. The General William Hart House in Old Saybrook has been restored, and a garden planted with fruit trees and 125 different herbs used in cooking and healing planted. Old Lyme, too, was a ship building and trading center.

Newport, Providence, Bristol, Warren and other towns in Rhode Island had excellent harbors and were centers of trade by the 1650s. Products included flour, wool, dried fish, beef, butter, horses, lumber, and fine clocks, silver and furniture, especially from Newport. The West Indies and Charleston were major trading partners importing molasses, sugar cane, spices and slaves. Rum and other goods were then traded in England and the West Indies, part of the "Triangular Trade". Later John Brown and others became involved in the China trade. James DeWolf of Bristol also owned a sugar plantation, and continued to import slaves well into the 1800s, even though there were federal laws prohibiting their importation.

Thomas Rogers settled in Old Orchard Beach, ME in 1657 as his "Garden by the Sea". The town received its name from the apple trees planted above the beach. Portland became a port and shipping center. Today, much of Maine's fish catch is unloaded here, with a public fish auction Monday to Thursday at 1:00. Along the Damariscotta River oyster shells were found thirty feet deep with implements used by the Native Americans. The Native Americans were thought to have summered along the banks of the river, fishing and digging oysters, which they smoked or dried for the winter. The oyster catch ran out a number of years ago, but seems to be making a comeback.

William Hickling Prescott, (1796-1859) occupied 55 Beacon Street, Boston. He was blinded in one eye during a food fight while a student at Harvard. He went on to memorize prose which he write down and went on to write such books as *The Reign of Ferdinand and Isabella.*

Faneuil Hall, Boston is the third building on this site, the first constructed in 1742, with funds from Peter Faneuil, a slave trader who thought the city should have a central market. The second building was completed in 1763 and was later used as a theater by the British. Nearby is the Quincy Market which opened in 1826 and was restored by James Rouse in 1975 and the Union Oyster House. The North and South Market, designed by Alexander Parris was built in the mid 1820s.

The Brazer Building, 27 State Street, Boston, was once the site of the Bunch of Grapes Tavern, where some of the revolutionaries met during the Revolution.

The House of Representatives at the State House, Boston contains the Sacred Codfish, a gilded fish representing the staple of the first settlers and also an important export. The cornerstone of the State House was laid in 1795.

The cookbook *The Frugal Housewife* was published in Boston in 1772 by Susanna Carter.

As wealth in this region increased more items, particularly British were imported into the colonies. The colonists resented taxation without representation and the Tea Tax brought about the infamous "Boston Tea Party" on December 16, 1773. Over two hundred men dumped three shiploads of tea in the Boston harbor. King George III closed the port and sent in troops. The British Parliament passed the Boston Port Bill in 1774. The bill forbade the landing of food and fuel in Boston until the East India Company was indemnified by Massachusetts for the tea thrown overboard.

Trade with Asia revived New England's economy following the Revolutionary War. The colonists imported porcelains, spices, silks that adorned the homes of even New England's staunchest Quakers. The *Grand Turk*, owned by Elias Haskett Derby of Salem, Ma was the first ship to leave for Canton in 1785.

From 1790 to 1959 Hancock Village, Pittsfield, MA was a Shaker farm. Today herb and vegetable gardens still flourish on its 1200 acres. Livestock common to 19th c Massachusetts is raised. Another Shaker farm open to the public is Canterbury Shaker Village in New Hampshire.

Jean-Baptiste-Gilbert Payplat dis Julien opened a restaurant in Boston by at the corner of Milk and Congress Streets in 1792. He introduced French favorites such as fondue, truffles from Perigord, and clear soup called consomme Julien. While staying in the United States Jean-Anthelme Brillat-Savarin, the famous French chef visited the restaurant.

Amelia Simmons published the first American cookbook *American Cookery, or The Art of Dressing Viands, Fish, Poultry, and Vegetables, and the Best Modes of Making Pastes, Puffs, Pies, Tarts, Puddings, Custards & Preserves, and All Kinds of Cakes, from the imperial Plumb to Plain Cake, adopted to this Country & All Grades of Life* in Hartford.

Frederick Tudor of Boston began to develop a method of transporting ice to the tropics and other warm places in 1805. With ice, fish and other foods could be shipped safely for long periods, earning him the title "The Ice King". His home once stood at 34 ½ Beacon Street. In 1825 Nathaniel Jervis Wyeth, an associate, patented an improved ice-making method. Sawdust was used to insulate the blocks of ice. The first cargo of ice left Boston for India in 1833 and took 4 months and 3 days. Also on board were apples, cheese and butter for the East India Company. One day while observing the ice harvesters cutting ice for shipment to India, Henry David Thoreau wrote "The pure Walden water is mingled with the sacred water of the Ganges."

The Thompson Ice House, Bristol, ME was used from 1826-1986 when ice was harvested from the local pond. Ice was shipped out of the country, packed in sawdust. Maine once supplied over three million tons of ice a year.

Richard Henry Dana, (1815-1882), lived at 43 Chestnut Street, Boston. *In Two Years Before the Mast*, he wrote in chapter 3 "Six days shalt thou labor and do all thou art able, And on the seventh - holystone the decks and scrape the table."

In 1816 many Vermonters left the state when crops failed due to a foot of snow in June, and smaller snowfalls in July and August.

In 1816 Henry Hall of Dennis, MA discovered that cranberry vines grew better where the wind has blown a mat over the vines. Swamps were drained and commercial bogs grew common. Cranberries were first cultivated on Nantucket in 1857. Prior to 1959 234 acres of bogs were cultivated, the largest contiguous cranberry bog in the world. Now the bogs have been divided up to conserve water. Wooden scoops were originally used to pick the cranberries. Today the bogs are flooded, with the cranberries rising to the surface and pulled to the edge of the bog with wooden booms. They are then washed and loaded on to trucks, and shipped off island. Rte. 6 on Cape Cod is called the "Cranberry Highway". The Jericho House Museum in Dennis and the Harwich Historical Society in Harwich Port display of equipment used to cultivate cranberries. In 1930 the Cranberry Canners, a growers' cooperative, was formed when the Ocean Spray Preserving Company merged with the Cranberry Products Company, New Egypt and the A.D. Makepeace Company, Wareham, MA. Wisconsin Sales Company joined the cooperative in 1940 and Washington Oregon growers in 1941. In 1946 the name was changed to the National Cranberry Association.

John Conant of Vermont patented an iron cooking stove in 1819.

In 1822 William Underwood established the first U.S. spice grinding company in Boston. He had already opened a shop on Russia's Wharf where he made ground mustard from imported seeds.

In 1824 Alfred Crowley began producing Colby Cheese at Healdville, VT. Also in that year the Rhode Island red hen was introduced in Little Compton, RI by a sea captain. The hens produced brown eggs, supposedly preferred by New Englanders.

The Providence Arcade, Providence, RI is the oldest enclosed shopping mall and was built 1828 in the Greek Revival style.

The first recipe for tomato ketchup appeared in 1830 in *the New England Farmer*.

Samuel Stillman Pierce opened the S.S. Pierce Co. in Boston in1831. Also in that year the Gorham and Webster Co. of Providence introduced table silver. The author's ancestor William Hadwen was one of Mr. Gorham's first partners before moving to Nantucket and entering the whaling business.

In 1836 a phosphorous match was patented by Alonzo D. Phillips of Springfield, MA that would later be used to light stoves and fires. In 1837 Vermonter John Deere of Grand Detour, IL built a self-polishing steel plow to break sod. The Deere Company was to become the major supplier of farm equipment. Also that year John A. Pitts and Hiram Abial Pitts of Winthrop, ME patented the first steam-powered threshing machine that could separate grain from straw and chaff.

Durgin-Park's Market Dining Room opened over a warehouse near the Faneuil and Quincy markets in 1840. The restaurant was known for serving guests at tables of ten, no matter the number in the party.

Oliver Chase, a Boston confectioner, invented the first automatic lozenge cutter in 1847. Also that year, Hanson Crockett Gregory of Camden, ME made the first ring doughnuts by cutting out the center of doughnuts and frying them separately. Mr. Chase received a patent for a machine to produce powdered sugar in 1851. But his real success came with slogans printed on the candies and NECCO Wafers. In 1900 the New England Confectionery Company (NECCO) was formed after the merger of three companies, including Oliver Chase's lozenge company. The Bolster bar made with peanut crunch covered with milk chocolate was introduced in 1930. In 1937 the Sky Bar was the first U.S. made molded chocolate bar with four centers – English toffee, honey nougat, nut butter toffee, and fudge parfait.

In 1853 Mrs. J. Chadwick of Boston wrote "Home Cookery" which included cake, meat and soup recipes.

In 1854 Daniel Forbes, a Boston candy maker, paid a missionary $125 for the recipe of "Turkish Delight". He made pralines by boiling nuts in brown sugar or maple syrup. In 1867 Mr. Forbes advertised mocha, a combination of powdered coffee and powdered cocoa.

William F. Schrafft founded Schrafft's Candy in Boston in 1861. Among the candies he produced were gumdrops, peppermint sticks, and cinnamon balls. The first Schrafft's Restaurant opened in New York City in 1897 and a Boston restaurant in 1928. In 1929 the company merged with the Frank Shattuck Company.

In the 1870s Chester Greenwood, a 15 year boy from Maine invented Greenwood's Champion Ear Protectors (ear muffs). He later went on to invent a cotton picker, washing machine, folding bed, and a doughnut hook.

In 1870 Margaret E. "Mattie" Knight obtained a patent for an attachment to bag-folding machines that produced a square bottom bag, similar to what is in the markets now.

In 1870 the first U.S. food trademark, number 82, was registered by the U.S. Patent Office to William Underwood & Co. of Boston for "deviled entremets". In 1881 William Underwood & Co. founded a sardine company at West Jonesport, ME. The sardines were fried in oil and packed with French names. In 1905 company employee Arthur R. Rogers received a patent for a machine to separate the fish by size and cleaning.

In 1871 the first load of bananas landed in Boston on board the *Telegraph* out of Kingston, Jamaica. Also that year John Blondell of Thomaston, ME was given a patent for a doughnut cutter.

In 1877 the first shipment of Chicago beef arrived in Boston sent in a special railcar by Gustavus Franklin Swift.

In 1880 Maria Parloa, director of the Boston Cooking School published Miss Parloa's "New Cook Book and Marketing Guide". In 1884 Mary Johnson Lincoln of the school published "Mrs. Lincoln's Boston Cook Book"and Maria Parloa published "Practical Cookery, with Demonstrations". Miss Parloa's next book " Miss Parloa's Kitchen Companion; a Guide for All who Would Be Housekeepers" came out in 1887 and in 1897 "One hundred Ways to Use Liebig's Extract of Beef; a Guide for American Housewifes".

In 1885 Andrew Preston and nine partners established the Boston Fruit Company to import bananas, later the United Fruit Company.

In 1889 Edward Williams Atkinson of Boston invented the slow-cooking Aladdin Oven.

In 1890 Ellen Swallow Richards and Mary Hinman Abel opened the New England Kitchen serving nutritious foods such as soups, stews, puddings, cakes and mush. In 1891 a bread annex opened. In 1892 the kitchen began to deliver hot lunches to a local school for 15 cents, and was later awarded a contract to supply all the Boston high schools. Fannie Merritt Farmer published "Fannie Farmer's Boston Cooking School cookbook" in 1896.

Mory's Tavern opened in New Haven in 1912 for use by students and professors.

In 1914 Charles N. Miller introduced Mary Janes, individually wrapped candies made from molasses and peanut butter. In 1919 a molasses tank exploded in Boston killing at least 13 people and poured out over 2.3 million gallons of molasses. Penick & Ford first started producing Brer Rabbit Molasses and Vermont Maid Maple Syrup in 1921 in New England. In 1965 R.J. Reynolds acquired the company. By then they were also producing My*T*Fine Pudding and Pie Fillings, and College Inn Chicken a la King.

During World War I Alice B. Kirk published in Boston "Practical Food Economy" which told cooks to "avoid fancy cooking"!!!!

In 1919 Peter Paul Halajian and five friends founded the Peter Paul Manufacturing Company. The first candy bar contained coconut, fruit, nuts and chocolate and sold as Konabar. The Mounds bar debuted in 1922 and also contained coconut and bittersweet chocolate. A new facility for producing candies was built in Naugatuck, CT. In 1929 Peter Paul Candies acquired J.N. Collins who produced Walnettos, Honey Scotch and Butter Scotch Caramels. In 1947 Almond Joy was introduced and in 1948 Welch's Pom Poms. In 1966 Peter Paul purchased the Walter H. Johnson Candy Co. in Chicago, makers of the PowerHouse bar. In that year the Caravelle candy bar made from soft caramel, crisped rice, milk chocolate and Brazil nuts becomes a hit.

In 1919 The New England Vinegar Works, originally the Standard Vinegar Company, Somerville, MA introduced the Veryfine name brand. Other products included cider vinegar, apple juice, apple jelly and prune juice. In 1958 the company became New England Apple Products. By 1981 the company had its own vending machines. The name was changed to VeryFine Products in 1989 and moved to Westford, MA.

In 1921 the Silver Company, Meriden, CT produced the first stainless-steel flatware, mainly knives for the hotel business. Stainless steel flatware did not become popular until the 1930s.

In 1922 Robert Henry Winborne Welch, Jr. began selling fudge in Cambridge, MA. He founded Welch's Oxford Candy Company which sold 3 pieces Avalon fudge for a dime. The company was sold to the Daggett Chocolate Company in 1926. Mr. Welch began manufacturing Papa suckers, caramel on a stick, and opened a plant in Chicago that closed in 1928. He then opened a plant in Brooklyn while serving as an executive with the E. J. Brach & Sons company in Chicago. He returned to Boston to work for his brother's James O. Welch Company. They manufactured such brands as Welch's Frappe Bar, Welch's Brazil Nut Fudge, Welch's Pecan Penuche, and Welch's Coconut. The Papa sucker became the Sugar Daddy. Later additions were Sugar Babies made of soft caramel. By 1935 U.S. candy consumption reached 13.7 pounds per capita. In 1945 Welch's Junior Mints were introduced, named for the Broadway play "Junior Miss" which James Welch had attended. Robert Welch was not only involved with the candy company, but wrote several books which included "The Life of John Birch" and "The Politician", and founded the John Birch Society in 1958. In 1963 Nabisco acquired the James O. Welch Co.

In 1924 Boston doctors George Richards Minot and William Parry Murphy introduce the theory that eating liver would prevent and cure pernicious anemia. In 1926 Dr. Edwin J. Cohn of Harvard developed an oral liver extract remedy.

In 1926 the Ginter Company of Boston merged with the O'Keefe and John T. Connor Companies to form the First National Stores.

In 1929 Rose and Sarkis Colombosian founded Colombo Yogurt in Andover, MA. In 1977 the company was purchased by Bongrain.and in 1978 began producing the first nonfat plain yogurt. Nonfat Light Yogurt with fruity flavors was introduced in 1988. In 1993 General Mills acquired Colombo

In 1938 Dewey and Almy of Boston founded the Cryovac deep-freezing method for food preservation.

Frances Roth, a lawyer and Katharine Angell, the wife of a former Yale president founded the Culinary Institute of America in New Haven in 1946. In 1947 the school moved to an estate outside New Haven and was renamed the Culinary Institute of Connecticut. The name was changed to

Culinary Institute of America in 1952 and in 1972 opened in Hyde Park, NY.

In 1947 Raytheon Co., Waltham, MA introduced the first commercial microwave oven. The Radarange restaurant oven cost $3,000.

In 1971 Madeleine Kamman published "The Making of a Cook". In 1975 she opened Madeleine Kamman's School of Traditional Cuisine and later the Modern Gourmet Cooking School and Restaurant, Newton Center, MA. In 1973 she published "Dinner Against the Clock".

In 1972 The Spa on Harvard Square introduced soft-frozen yogurt.

In 1978 Cuisinart, Inc. of Greenwich, CT introduced the DLC series of food processors. The Cuisinart food processors were first manufactured in 1973.

In 1980 "Cook's" magazine began publication in Westport, CT. Christopher Kimball, the publisher later introduced "Cook's Illustrated".

HISTORIC INNS AND TAVERNS

The White Horse Tavern in Newport, RI was built in 1673 and is the oldest continually operated tavern in the United States. The Moorings Restaurant is on the site of the summer New York Yacht Club. The Whitehall Farm Museum was occupied by Bishop George Berkeley from 1729-31. During his tenure the house was enlarged and eventually given to Yale to provide revenue for scholarships. The house has been used as a tearoom, tavern and bunkhouse for the British soldiers during the Revolution. Today the house is maintained by the Colonial Dames. The Redwood Library was named in honor of Abraham Redwood, a wealthy merchant and owner of sugar plantations in Antigua, who donated 500 pounds for the library.

The John Paul Jones House, Portsmouth, NH was built in 1758. John Paul Jones stayed here in 1782 while his ship *America* was being readied. At that time the home was run as an inn by Sarah Purcell.

The Wyman Tavern, Keene, NH was built in 1762 for Isaac Wyman and in 1770 was the site of the founding meeting for Dartmouth College.

Thayer's Hotel in Littleton, NH is one of the states oldest inns dating to 1848.

In the 1880s Augustus Saint-Gaudens, the sculptor, rented an inn, Huggins Folly, built in 1805, in Cornish, NH. Later he bought the property which is now the Saint-Gaudens National Historic Site.

The Wallomsac Inn, Bennington, VT was built in 1766 by Elijah Dewey. During the Battle of Bennington British and Hessian soldiers were brought here for their meals. The Peter Matteson Tavern dates from the 1780s. The Munro-Hawkins House was built in 1808 for Joshua Munro who exported wheat to France during the Napoleonic Wars and is now an inn.

The Eagle Tavern, Poultney, VT was a 1785 stagecoach inn. Horace Greeley, founder of the *New York Times*, apprenticed at *the Northern Spectator* and often stayed here.

The Chimney Point Tavern, Larrabee's Point, VT is on the site overlooking Lake Champlain that Samuel de Champlain gave his name to the lake in 1609. In 1690 the French built a fort here, and later Benjamin Paine built the tavern. During the Revolution both British and American soldiers frequented the tavern. Today the tavern is a museum.

The Old Constitution House, Windsor, VT is an 18th c tavern where representatives met in 1777 to adopt Vermont's constitution which was signed on the tavern table, still on display. The Equinox Inn, Manchester, dates to 1769 and sits on 2300 acres. Ethan Allen and the Green Mountain Boys once hung out at the Marsh Tavern and at the Catamount Tavern in Bennington, VT.

Shelburne Farms, VT, a working farm museum, was developed by William Seward Webb, in 1886. Vermont cheddar is produced here.

The Horn of the Moon Café, Montpelier, VT claims to be the oldest vegetarian natural foods restaurant in New England.

The Jefferds Tavern, York, ME was built in 1750 for Captain Samuel Jefferds Among the house rules, guests were admonished "to abhor all oaths, curses and blasphemy". The Emerson-Wilcox House has been a post office, tavern, tailor's shop and private residence.

In 1775 townspeople gathered at the Burnham Tavern, Machias, ME, built in 1770, to plan attacks against the British.

The Nickels-Sortwell, Wicasset, ME was built in 1805 for Captain William Nickels whose fortune was made through lumber and shipping. After his death the house was known as Turner's Tavern.

The Captain Fairfield Inn, Kennebunkport, ME is a Federal style home built c1813 for James Fairfield, a sea captain and privateer. Also built in 1813 is the Black Hawk Putnam Tavern in Houlton. Houlton was a market town in the 1890s.

The Agamont House inn, Bar Harbor, ME opened in 1855, changing the economy from fishing and shipbuilding to tourism.

Craignair Inn, Spruce Head, ME was built in 1928 to house workers from the nearby quarries. In 1940 the building was converted to an inn.

The Red Lion Inn, Stockbridge, MA, built in 1773 on the Albany Boston post road, burned in 1896, but was rebuilt almost immediately. The artist Norman Rockwell lunched at the inn every Thursday. Joe's Diner in Lee was the setting for Rockwell's painting, *The Runaway*.

A plaque marks the site of the Cooper Tavern once located at Medford Street and Massachusetts Avenue in Arlington, MA where two men were killed by British soldiers on April 18, 1775 after Paul Revere and William Dawes galloped through the town. Nearby was the site of the Black Horse Tavern where the British raided a meeting of the Committee of Safety and Supplies.

In Lexington, MA the Minute Men who had mustered during Paul Revere's alarm at Buckman Tavern waited for the Regulars to arrive. Sergeant William Munroe, owner of Munroe Tavern and one of the Minute Men, stood guard at the Hancock-Clarke House where John Hancock and Samuel Adams were staying that night. Lord Percy, the commander of the British relief column set up his field headquarters here. After the bartender poured drinks for the British officers, he tried to flee and was shot in the back. A bullet hole can still be seen in the ceiling. A field headquarters was also set up by the British at Wright's Tavern in Concord.

The Fruitlands Museum near Concord was set up in 1843 as a communal farm by Amos Bronson Alcott, father of Louisa May Alcott, and Charles Lane. The farm was disbanded in 1844 and the Alcott's moved back to Concord.

The Wayside Inn, Sudbury, MA, built in 1700 was the gathering point for the Sudbury militia before heading off to the Battle of Lexington. The inn was made famous in Henry Wadsworth Longfellow's *Tales of a Wayside Inn*. The inn was purchased in 1923 by Henry Ford who restored the inn and added a reconstructed gristmill.

The Store at Five Corners, Williamstown, MA dates to 1770 and was a country store. Today the store sells sandwiches and baked goods. In 1967 Arlo Guthrie wrote "Alice's Restaurant", a song about a restaurant in Stockbridge, MA run by Alice and Ray Brock who had been his schoolteachers.

In 1973 the Harvest restaurant opened at 44 Brattle Street, Boston. The first chef is Bob Kincaid, followed by Lydia Shire. Ms. Shire opened Biba in 1989, the same year Olives opened.

Jasper White opened Jasper's in 1984 at 240 Commercial Street, Boston and published "Jasper White's Cooking from New England" in 1989.

The King's Rook café and wine bar, Marblehead, MA dates to 1747.

The Inn on Cove Hill, Rockport, MA, was built in 1791 with pirates' gold found at Gully Point.

The Edgartown Inn was built as a home for Thomas Worth in 1798. The Daggett House Restaurant, also in Edgartown, was built c1730.

The Jared Coffin House on Nantucket was built in 1845 for a ship owner. The house was the first three story mansion on the island, and today is considered

The Wedgewood Inn Yarmouthport dates to 1812 and is on the National Register of Historic Places. Also on Cape Cod is the Wingscorton Farm Inn in Sandwich with the house dating to 1758.

The Harborside Inn, Boston was built in 1858 as a spice warehouse. It is now a boutique hotel in the financial district. The Warren Tavern c 1780 is one of the oldest restaurants in Boston.

The Ritz Hotel, opened in 1927, and the Copley Hotel are the grande dames of Boston hotels. They have been the sites of some of the most formal parties – debutante parties, and Waltz Evenings where ladies still where long gloves and gentlemen tails. Elegant dinner parties precede these events, often with many course meals that are quickly danced off. The Hotel Vendome opened in Boston at the corner of Commonwealth Avenue and Darmouth Street in 1872. Its dining room could seat 320 people.

In 1876 Locke-Obers Restaurant opened at 3 and 4 Winter Place and was named Frank Locke's Winter Place Wine Rooms.

Howard Johnson's restaurants were founded in Orleans, MA in 1936 by Reginald Sprague. Howard Johnson supplied the restaurants with ice cream, fried clams and frankfurters. The restaurants were franchised beginning in 1937. By 1960 Howard Johnson had 607 independently owned restaurants.

Joyce Chen opened the first Mandarin restaurant in New England in 1958 in Cambridge. In 1962 she published "The Joyce Chen Cookbook".

Anthony Athanas opened the Pier Four restaurant in Boston in 1960.

The Old Ordinary, Hingham, MA dates to the 17th c and had been a tavern. Today it is the Historical Society's house museum.

The Candleworks Restaurant in New Bedford, MA was built in 1810 as a spermaceti candle factory.

The Parker House Hotel opened in Boston in 1855. The hotel served meals at any hour. The Parker House roll received its name from the hotel.

The Wiggins Tavern at the Hotel Northampton in Holyoke, MA has been operating as a tavern since 1876.

Sturbridge, MA is a recreated New England village producing its own vegetables, herbs, lambs, calves, pumpkins, apples and other staples. The Wight House was built c1789 and served as a tavern and roadside lodging.

La Boniche restaurant in Lowell, MA is located in the Bon Marche building built in 1892, once Lowell's most prominent store fashioned in the Beaux Arts style. The Old Worthern Tavern is Lowell's oldest tavern, located in a building dating back to the 1830s.

General Israel Putnam was staying at Knapp's Tavern, Greenwich, CT during the Revolution when the British Dragoons appeared. Tales of his jumping over a cliff on his horse live on in legend. Today the site is Putnam Cottage. The Bush-Holley House, built in the 1730s and once owned by David Bush, was purchased by Edward and Josephine Holley in 1882 and converted into a boarding house. The house attracted many artists from New York. Later the inn was run by their daughter Emma Holley and her sculptor husband, Elmer Livingston MacRae.

The Griswold Inn, Essex, CT, built in 1776 has been used continuously as an inn or tavern. Nearby is Hill's Academy Museum, once Hill's Academy, a school built in 1832 and supported by Joseph Hill, who donated about $600 a year from his shad fishery business.

The Leffingwell Inn, Norwich, CT was a meeting place during the Revolution. Christopher Leffingwell not only maintained the inn, but a ship brokerage, stoneware kiln, stocking factory, a potash works, a store, dye house, and the first papermill in Connecticut. His chocolate factory produced over five thousand pounds of chocolate a year. During the Revolution Mr. Leffingwell provided the American troops with bread, flour, salt pork and other foodstuffs. He was never repaid by Congress and at the end of the war was left penniless.

The Bates-Schofield Homestead, Darien, CT dating from 1736, has been restored with a kitchen and buttery, weaving room, and colonial herb garden.

The Keeler Tavern, Ridgefield, CT still has a cannonball lodged in its wall from the British bombardment of the town. The inn was a summer home for fifty years to Cass Gilbert, the architect.

The Silvermine Tavern, Norwalk, CT dates to 1785. The author remembers meeting her grandparents here for lunch as they traveled to and from Nantucket.

The Butler-McCook Homestead, Hartford, CT has a kitchen dating back to 1782 The house was operated as a blacksmith and butcher shop, and is now open to the public.

APPETIZERS

The author's mother, Mrs. William Hadwen Barney and grandmother,
Mrs. Grafton Sherwood Kennedy, Women's City Club, Boston in 1939

On January 1, 1802 a 1,235 pound cheese was delivered to Thomas Jefferson at the White House by a man from Cheshire, MA. Inscribed on the cheese were the words "the greatest cheese in America for the greatest man in America". The cheese was served at a New Year's Day reception in the East Room.

GRILLED SEA SCALLOPS

2 pounds sea scallops   Juice of 2 limes

- In a bowl marinate the scallops in the lime juice for two hours.
- Grill on a barbecue until just browned.
- Place on a round tray and serve with the green apple chutney or pesto cream.
- Mussels or oysters can be substituted for the scallops

Green Apple Chutney

12 green apples, peeled, cored and chopped

3 green tomatoes, chopped

2 cups currants

1 red onion, chopped

3 cups brown sugar

1 Tbls. kosher salt

2 cups cider vinegar

2 Tbls. fresh grated ginger

3 jalapenos, seeded and chopped

¼ teaspoon cayenne

1 teaspoon allspice

1 ½ teaspoons mustard seeds

- Combine all ingredients in a large pot. Bring to a boil and then simmer until apples, tomatoes and onions are tender, about ½ hour. Pour into a bowl.
- This will make plenty for later use to serve with ham or other dishes. Refrigerate.

Pesto Cream

2 bunches fresh basil, remove stems

3 large cloves garlic

¼ cup pine nuts

½ cup Pecorino Romano cheese

¼ cup virgin olive oil

1 teaspoon fresh ground pepper

1 cup heavy cream

- In a food processor combine the basil, garlic, pine nuts, cheese, olive oil and pepper.
- Pour into a bowl and stir in the cream.

SCALLOP PUFFS

1 loaf thin sliced bread, cut with biscuit cutter into small circles

½ stick butter, melted
2 pounds bay scallops
Grated rind and juice of 1 lemon
¼ cup fresh dill, chopped

½ pound fresh grated parmesan cheese
2 cups mayonnaise

- ♦ In a bowl combine all the ingredients. Spread on top of each circle.

BOURBON SCALLOPS

2 dozen sea scallops

12 slices maple bacon

- ♦ Cut the bacon slices in half. Wrap around the scallop.
- ♦ Place on a cookie sheet and set under broiler until just browned.
- ♦ Serve with bourbon sauce or aoli.

Bourbon Sauce

¼ cup bourbon
¼ cup chives, chopped

2 Tbls. Lemon juice

- ♦ Combine bourbon, lemon juice and chives in a sauce pan. Heat until reduced to ½.
- ♦ Pour over scallops after they have been placed on a serving platter.

Aioli

4 garlic cloves, peeled
2 egg yolks
1 teaspoon sea salt
1 cup virgin olive oil

1 teaspoon Dijon mustard
½ teaspoon cold water
1 Tbls. lime juice
¼ cup basil

- ♦ Combine all ingredients in food processor until thickened.

OYSTERS AND SCALLOPS WITH CORN RELISH

2 dozen sea scallops
2 oysters
2 eggs, beaten

1 cup corn meal
Vegetable oil

- ◆ Grill the sea scallops on skewers on a BBQ until just browned.
- ◆ Dip oysters in beaten eggs and then in cornmeal.
- ◆ Heat oil in large skillet.
- ◆ Fry oysters until just browned. Drain on paper towels.

Corn Relish

4 cups fresh corn
2 avocados, peeled and diced
1 red bell pepper, chopped
2 green onions, chopped
1 large tomato, chopped

¼ cup vinegar
2 Tbl. olive oil
Salt and pepper to taste
¼ cup basil or cilantro, chopped

- ◆ Combine all ingredients in a bowl. Serve with scallops and oysters.

CLAM DIP

1 pound fresh chopped clams
3 cloves garlic, minced
8 ounces cream cheese
Juice of 1 lemon

1 teaspoon Worcestershire sauce
Dash of Tabasco
4 chives, snipped
½ cup toasted sunflower seeds

- ◆ Preheat oven to 350
- ◆ In a small baking dish combine clams, garlic, cream cheese, lemon juice, Worcestershire, Tabasco and chives. Top with sunflower seeds.
- ◆ Bake 15 minutes or until bubbling.

CLAM AND CHEDDAR TOASTS

1 loaf thin sliced bread, each slice cut into 2 triangles

2 dozen quahaugs
¼ cup olive oil
1 medium onion, chopped
2 cloves garlic, crushed

2 large tomatoes, chopped
¼ cup fresh basil chopped
½ pound grated cheddar cheese

- ◆ Preheat oven to 350°.
- ◆ Place the clams on a baking tray and place in oven until the clams open.
- ◆ Remove clams from the shell, reserving the liquid. Chop the clams.
- ◆ In a skillet heat the olive oil and add onions stirring until transparent. Add the garlic and tomatoes, stirring until tender. Add the basil and clams.
- ◆ Turn the oven up to broil.
- ◆ Place the bread triangles on a cookie sheet and put under broiler until just golden on each side.
- ◆ Top each of the triangles with some of the clam mixture. Top with the grated cheese.
- ◆ Place under broiler until bubbling and the cheese is melted.
- ◆ Serve on a tray garnished with fresh basil leaves.

STUFFED CLAMS

2 dozen clams
4 cloves garlic, minced
¼ cup parsley, chopped
4 green onion, chopped

¼ cup white wine
1 Tbls. oregano, chopped
¼ cup lemon juice

- ◆ Preheat oven to 350
- ◆ Put clams on cookie sheet. Bake until clams open. Remove 1 shell.
- ◆ Chop clams.
- ◆ In a bowl combine clams, garlic, parsley, onion, wine, oregano and lemon juice.
- ◆ Stuff clams with mixture.
- ◆ Bake for 10 minutes or until bubbling.
- ◆ 1 cup bread crumbs can also be added to mixture.

CLAMS CASINO

4 dozen quahaugs
2 red bell peppers, diced
2 green peppers, diced
1 red onion, chopped
12 slices bacon
2 cups croutons

½ teaspoon cayenne
1 teaspoon salt
1 teaspoon pepper
1 Tbls. oregano
¼ cup fresh basil

- Preheat oven to 350°.
- In a skillet fry the bacon until crisp. Remove from skillet and crumble.
- Add vegetables to skillet and cook until tender. Add croutons and seasonings.
- Place clams on a cookie sheet and bake until clams just open.
- Remove from oven and discard top shell from each clam. Top clams with vegetable/bacon mixture.
- Bake for 15-20 minutes or until golden brown.
- Bread crumbs can be substituted for croutons.

STUFFED CLAMS II

2 dozen quahaugs
2 Tbls. olive oil
¼ cup shallots chopped
2 garlic cloves, chopped
½ pound mushrooms, chopped
2 medium tomatoes, chopped

¼ cup fresh basil, chopped
4 slices bacon, cooked and crumbled
Salt and pepper
¼ teaspoon cayenne
1 cup fresh bread crumbs

- Preheat oven to 350°.
- Place the clams on a cookie sheet and bake until the shells just open. Remove from oven and remove top shell. Chop the clams. In a bowl put the clams and their liqueur.
- In a skillet saute the shallots in the olive oil. Add garlic, mushrooms, tomatoes and basil. Season with salt, pepper, and cayenne. Add bacon and clams and liqueur.
- In remaining shells stuff the clams. Top with bread crumbs.
- Place under broiler until just bubbling.

SPINACH STUFFED CLAMS

2 dozen quahaugs
½ pound fresh baby spinach
¼ cup olive oil
¼ cup pine nuts

½ pound Gorgonzola cheese
1 cup roasted peppers (2 large peppers roasted in oven or store bought)

- ◆ Preheat oven to 350°.
- ◆ Place the clams on a cookie sheet and place in oven until shells are just opened. Open the clams and remove one shell. Dispose of extra shell.
- ◆ In a skillet heat the olive oil and stir in spinach until just wilted. Remove from the heat.
- ◆ Add the pine nuts, Gorgonzola and roasted peppers.
- ◆ Spread this mixture on top of each clam in its shell.
- ◆ Bake in oven 15-20 minutes or until bubbly.

SEAFOOD SKEWERS

2 dozen sea scallops
2 dozen shrimp, cooked, peeled and deveined

½ cup lime juice

- ◆ In a bowl marinate the scallops and shrimp in lime juice for at least two hours in refrigerator.
- ◆ Place shrimp and scallops on skewers.
- ◆ Grill for about 5 minutes on each side, or until just browned.
- ◆ Remove from skewers.
- ◆ Serve on a fish platter with bowl of spicy coconut sauce.

Spicy Coconut Cream Sauce

1 cup coconut milk
2 cloves garlic, minced
¼ cup red onion, finely chopped

¼ cup cilantro, chopped
¼ teaspoon cayenne
2 T. fresh grated ginger

- ◆ Combine ingredients in a bowl.

SMOKED BLUEFISH

1 pound smoked bluefish, broken into small pieces
8 ounces cream cheese
½ cup sour cream

Juice of 1 lemon
1 green onion, chopped
2 Tbls. horseradish
2 Tbls. dill

- ◆ Combine all the ingredients in a bowl.
- ◆ Serve with crackers or French bread.

GRILLED MUSSELS

2 dozen mussels in shell
Pesto – p. 31

4 cloves garlic, minced
½ stick butter, softened

- ◆ Grill mussels on BBQ until shells just open. Remove one shell.
- ◆ In a bowl combine garlic and butter.
- ◆ Top mussels with a small amount of pesto and garlic butter.

SALMON ASPARAGUS WRAP

1 pound thin asparagus
1 bunch fresh basil leaves

½ pound smoked salmon

- ◆ In a sauce pan blanche the asparagus for 3 minutes.
- ◆ Wrap a piece of the salmon around the asparagus and several of the basil leaves. Hold with a toothpick.
- ◆ Serve on a platter garnished with basil leaves.

SMOKED SALMON BLINI

1 pound smoked salmon
½ cup sour cream

1 small jar salmon caviar
Blini

♦ Place a small piece of the smoked salmon on each blini. Top with sour cream and a dollop of the caviar.
♦ At Christmas this is very pretty served with a parsley leaf for color.

Blini

½ stick butter
1 cup milk
1 egg
1 cup flour

2 Tbls. fresh tarragon, chopped
2 Tbls. chives, snipped
2 Tbls. basil, chopped

♦ Combine all the ingredients in a bowl.
♦ Heat a skillet. Melt a small amount of butter to keep from sticking. Drop batter by teaspoon to make quarter size blini.
♦ Place on serving dish.

SMOKED TROUT WITH HERB SOUR CREAM AND FRUIT CHUTNEY

1 loaf French bread, sliced
1 pound smoked trout
Fruit Chutney, p. - 204

2 Tbls. fresh basil, chopped
½ cup sour cream

♦ In a bowl combine the basil and sour cream. Spread a small amount of mixture on each slice of bread.
♦ Put a small piece of smoked trout on each slice of bread.
♦ Top with chutney.

TUNA BLINI WITH SALSA

2 pounds tuna
Cornmeal blini

Salsa
Sour cream

- ◆ Grill the tuna on a barbecue. Cut into bite size pieces.
- ◆ Serve on blini topped with salsa and a dab of sour cream.

Cornmeal Blini

½ cup cornmeal
½ cup flour
1 egg
1 teaspoon baking powder

½ teaspoon salt
1 cup milk
2 Tbls. sour cream
2 Tbls. melted butter

- ◆ In a bowl combine the ingredients.
- ◆ Heat a skillet and drop the dough by tablespoons to make silver dollar size blini. Brown on each side.

Onion and Tomato Salsa

1 small red onion, chopped finely
2 large tomatoes, chopped finely
2 jalapenos, seeded and chopped
2 Tbls. olive oil

¼ cup fresh cilantro, chopped
½ teaspoon kosher salt
1 teaspoon fresh ground pepper
2 Tbls. lemon or lime juice

- ◆ Combine all ingredients in a bowl.
- ◆ Corn can be substituted for the tomatoes.

Avocado Salsa

1 small red onion, chopped
1 large ripe avocado, peeled, seeded and diced
1 large tomato, diced
2 jalapenos, seeded and chopped

¼ cup sour cream
¼ cup cilantro, chopped
2 Tbls. Lemon or lime juice
½ teaspoon kosher salt

- ◆ Combine all ingredients in a bowl.

BAKED BRIE

1 small round brie
1 package crescent rolls
1 large apple peeled, seeded and
sliced thinly

½ pint raspberries
½ cup pecans
2 Tbls. butter

- ◆ Preheat oven to 425°.
- ◆ On a floured cutting board spread the crescent rolls into one large circle. Top with the brie.
- ◆ Place the apple slices in a circle on the brie. Top with raspberries and pecans.
- ◆ Fold the pastry around the brie. Seal at edges. Turn over so folded side is on bottom. Top with the butter.
- ◆ Bake 15-20 minutes until just browned.
- ◆ Serve with French bread or crackers.
- ◆ A variation of this is to just serve the brie, sliced in half. In center put apple slices and pecans. Top with raspberries. Do not warm.

PESTO BRIE

1 pound round of brie
Pesto

French bread, thinly sliced

Pesto

2 large bunches basil
½ cup pine nuts
½ cup olive oil

½ cup grated parmesan cheese
4 cloves garlic

- ◆ Remove the stems from the basil.
- ◆ Combine all the ingredients in a food processor.
- ◆ Slice the brie in half and spread the pesto between the layers.
- ◆ Serve with the French bread.

BRIE WITH MUSHROOMS

4 large strawberries, sliced
2 Tbls. balsamic vinegar
2 Tbls. sugar
2 Tbls. fresh orange juice
1 pound round of brie
2 Tbls. butter

½ pound of porcini mushrooms, sliced
1 Tbls. truffle oil
2 Tbls. butter
1 package refrigerator crescent rolls
French bread

- ◆ Preheat oven to 400°
- ◆ In a bowl combine the strawberries with the vinegar, sugar and orange juice.
- ◆ Melt 2 Tbls. of butter in a skillet and sauté the mushrooms. Drizzle the truffle oil over the mushrooms.
- ◆ Roll out the crescent rolls into a circle. Place the brie in the center of the circle. Top with the mushrooms. Fold the rolls around the brie. Turn brie upside down. Top with 2 Tbls. butter.
- ◆ Bake for 15-20 minutes or until golden. Remove from oven. Place on a serving dish.
- ◆ Top with the strawberry mixture.
- ◆ Serve with sliced French bread.

HERBED BAKED BRIE

1 round brie
1 package crescent rolls
2 Tbls, parsley, chopped
2 Tbs. basil, chopped

1 Tbls. rosemary
1 Tbls. thyme
½ stick butter, softened

- ◆ Preheat oven to 400
- ◆ Roll out the crescent rolls into a circle to fit around the brie.
- ◆ Top brie with herbs and ½ butter. Fold side of pastry around brie. Turn over and place in small baking dish. Put rest of butter on top.
- ◆ Bake 15-20 minutes, or until pastry is just browned.
- ◆ Serve garnished with more herbs, crackers, or toasted French toast.

BAKED BRIE WITH FRUIT

1 large round brie
1 pint fresh blueberries

1 pint fresh blackberries
1 pint fresh raspberries

- ♦ Heat oven to 400°.
- ♦ Place brie on a cookie sheet. Bake for 20 minutes. Remove and place on serving platter.
- ♦ Top with coulis and berries.
- ♦ Serve with crusty French bread.
- ♦ Can also be served without baking. Just cut in half. Place half of berries in center and half on top. Top with coulis.

Raspberry Coulis

1 pint raspberries

Zest of one orange

- ♦ In food processor combine the raspberries and zest. Serve over the brie.

BACON WRAPPED APPLES

4 large apples, cored and thickly sliced
½ pound bacon

½ pound whole blanched almonds
Maple Syrup

- ♦ Preheat broiler.
- ♦ Cut each slice of bacon into 3 pieces.
- ♦ Wrap each slice around the apple slice and an almond. Secure with a toothpick. Place on a cookie sheet. Drizzle with the maple syrup.
- ♦ Place under broiler turning apples until bacon is crisp.
- ♦ Dates, pears, peaches or apricots can be substituted for the apple slices.

STUFFED EGGS

Serves 8

8 eggs
¼ cup mayonnaise
1 teaspoon Dijon mustard

1 teaspoon anchovy paste
Paprika
Capers

- ◆ Hard boil eggs. Cool. Slice in half lengthwise.
- ◆ Remove yolk and place in bowl. Mash together with mayonnaise, Dijon mustard, and anchovy paste.
- ◆ Fill egg halves with mixture. Sprinkle with paprika. Garnish with capers

BLUE CHEESE CAKE

½ cup fine fresh bread crumbs
¼ cup fresh grated parmesan cheese
½ stick butter, melted
16 ounces cream cheese
4 large eggs

½ cup heavy cream
8 slices bacon
1 medium onion, chopped
½ pound blue cheese, crumbled
¼ teaspoon cayenne

- ◆ Preheat oven to 300°
- ◆ In a 10" round porcelain dish spread the bread crumbs and parmesan cheese. Add butter to bind.
- ◆ Combine the cream cheese, cream and eggs in a bowl.
- ◆ In a skillet saute the bacon until crisp. Remove and add onions. Cook until translucent.
- ◆ Add onion, bacon, blue cheese and cayenne to cream cheese mixture.
- ◆ Pour into crust. Bake 1 hour.
- ◆ Place on serving platter. Serve in slices with toasted French bread or crackers.

PITA PIZZA

6 pita bread pockets
3 large tomatoes
3 large scallions
¼ cup olive oil

1 cup chopped pitted black or
Kalamata olives
2 Tbls. fresh oregano, chopped
½ pound shredded Mozarella
cheese

♦ Preheat oven to 450°.
♦ Slice the pita in half for 12 little pita pizza crusts.
♦ Coarsely chop the tomatoes and scallions including the dark green parts and add the olive oil.
♦ Spoon the mixture onto the Pitas.
♦ Garnish with chopped black olives, oregano and Mozarella.
♦ Place on baking sheet(s) in oven until the cheese melts and the crusts begin to toast lightly.
♦ Serve warm or at room temperature. These can be sliced into bite-sized pieces for an easy appetizer or served with a salad as a main course.

CHEESE AND SPINACH PIES

8 ounces Mozarella cheese
2 Tbls. chopped mint
1 cup spinach
2 eggs, beaten

1 teaspoon fresh ground black
pepper
10 sheets phyllo pastry
2 sticks butter
Fresh parsley

♦ Preheat oven to 350°.
♦ Combine the first five ingredients in a food processor.
♦ Cut phyllo sheets into 2-3 inch squares. (Keep a damp tea towel to cover dough to prevent drying out).
♦ Melt the butter (or substitute olive oil) and brush on each dough square.
♦ Place teaspoon of spinach filling on square and fold into a triangle. Arrange triangles on backing sheet and brush with oil or butter.
♦ Bake in oven until golden brown.
♦ Garnish with fresh parsley leaves

SPINACH DIP

1 cup mayonnaise
1 cup sour cream
2 green onions, chopped
¼ cup fresh parsley

1 pound fresh baby spinach
2 Tbls. basil, chopped
2 Tbls. dill, chopped
1 round loaf unsliced herb bread

- ◆ Put all ingredients, except bread, in a food processor until just combined.
- ◆ Cut out a round hole in top of bread. Scoop out bread with spoon.
- ◆ Spoon spinach mixture into bread.
- ◆ Serve with bread pieces.

SPINACH SQUARES

Makes 18 squares

1 pound fresh spinach, chopped
1 medium onion, chopped
¼ cup olive oil
2 cloves garlic, chopped
4 eggs
¼ cup bread crumbs
½ teaspoon oregano

½ teaspoon pepper
½ teaspoon salt
¼ cup fresh parsley, chopped
Dash of Tabasco or cayenne
2 cups grated fresh parmesan cheese

- ◆ Preheat oven to 350°.
- ◆ In a skillet saute the spinach, onion, and garlic until just tender.
- ◆ In a large bowl beat the eggs, and add the bread crumbs, salt, pepper, oregano, Tabasco, parsley, and cheese. Stir in the spinach mixture.
- ◆ Pour into a 9" x 13" baking pan greased with olive oil. Bake for 30 minutes and until just browned and set. Let cool and cut into squares.
- ◆ This can be served hot or cold as an appetizer or side vegetable dish.
- ◆ One pound fresh chopped broccoli or a 15 ounce can of chopped artichoke hearts can be substituted for the spinach. Fresh basil can be substituted for the parsley.

HERB DIP

1 cup mayonnaise
1 cup sour cream
2 Tbls. fresh dill
2 Tbls. fresh tarragon

2 cloves garlic, crushed
2 Tbls. chives, snipped
2 Tbls. parsley, chopped
Salt and pepper

- ◆ Combine all ingredients in a bowl.
- ◆ Serve in a bowl.
- ◆ Serve with fresh vegetables or sliced French bread.

APPLE DIP

8 ounces cream cheese
1 cup brown sugar
2 Tbls. rum

½ cup chopped pecans or walnuts
4 apples, sliced

- ◆ Combine the cream cheese, brown sugar, rum, and nuts in a bowl.
- ◆ Serve with apple slices.

CUCUMBER DIP

3 cups plain yogurt or sour cream
2 small to medium cucumbers, peeled
4 cloves garlic
1 teaspoon salt

1 tablespoon red wine vinegar
3 Tbls. olive oil
¼ cup fresh dill, chopped
5 radishes, sliced
1 small cucumber, sliced
5 black olives, sliced

- ◆ Blend together first six ingredients in food processor. Chill.
- ◆ Place in a bowl. Garnish with thin radish slices, chopped dill, thin cucumber slices, and black olives sliced thin
- ◆ Sour cream can be substituted for the yogurt.
- ◆ Pita wedges, broccoli florets, baby carrots, or any kind of interesting bread sticks or chips can be used for serving with the dip.

STUFFED MUSHROOM CAPS

3 dozen mushroom caps   ½ cup bread crumbs
1 container Boursin

- Preheat oven to 375°.
- Clean the mushroom caps. Stuff with boursin.
- Sprinkle with bread crumbs. Bake for 15 minutes or until just bubbling.

PORTABELLA MUSHROOMS WITH SPINACH

This can be served as an appetizer or side dish.

1 pound small portabella mushrooms, stems removed and saved   ½ pound fresh baby spinach
1 red pepper, roasted, finely chopped

- Preheat oven to 350°.
- In a bowl combine the spinach and roasted pepper. Stuff into the mushroom caps.
- Pour the mushroom sherry sauce over each mushroom.
- Bake for 15 minutes or until mushrooms are just tender.

Mushroom Sherry Sauce

¼ cup sherry   Mushroom stems, finely chopped
2 Tbls. butter

- Combine the ingredients in a sauce pan. Heat until the butter is melted.

CHUTNEY CHEESE DIP

8 ounces cream cheese
1 jar cranberry chutney (p. 202)
½ cup toasted almonds

French bread, toasted and sliced,
or ginger snaps

- ♦ Mound the cream cheese on a serving dish. Top with cranberry chutney and almonds.
- ♦ Serve with French bread or ginger snaps.

ORANGE CHEESE SPREAD

½ pound Gouda cheese
3 oz. cream cheese
¼ cup orange juice

Zest of 1 orange
1 Tbls. sugar
½ cup dried apricots, chopped

- ♦ Place all ingredients in food processor until just combined.
- ♦ Serve with ginger snaps.

BEEF BALLS

1 pound ground beef
1 egg
1 cup blue cheese
½ cup bread crumbs

2 cloves garlic, minced
½ teaspoon salt
½ teaspoon pepper
Bacon

- ♦ Preheat oven to 400°
- ♦ Combine all ingredients except bacon in a bowl. Shape into small balls.
- ♦ Cut each slice of bacon in two and wrap around each ball.
- ♦ Bake in oven for 25 minutes or until bacon is crisp.
- ♦ Serve with cranberry chutney.

SPECIAL DRINKS

"Root Beer Sold Here". It seemed to me the perfection of pith and pity."
The Story of a Bad Boy
Thomas Bailey Aldrich, former editor of the *Atlantic Monthly*, Boston
(1836-1907)

Cousin Marge (Mrs. David Swain) and the author's mother at the
Barnacle

In 1631 lemon juice was brought by ship to Boston, where scurvy and other diseases had affected many of the early colonists.

In 1750 Massachusetts had 63 distilleries to produce rum made from molasses, about 1500 hogsheads a year.

On March 2, 1775 Providence had its own tea party when the Gaspe went aground off Warwick. Patriots brought some of the tea ashore and burned it in Market Square. Rhode Island declared independence on May 4, 1776, two months before the other colonies.

In 1845 Poland Spring Water was first bottled at Poland Spring, ME by Hiram Ricker

In 1851 Maine Law prohibited the making and selling of alcohol in the state, the first law in the U.S. prohibiting production. Portland was known for its prosperous rum trade. Neal Dow, a brigadier general in the Civil War, mayor of Portland, state legislator and presidential candidate on the Prohibition ticket initiated the law. His son later gave his home, the Neal Dow Memorial in Portland, to the Maine Women's Christian Temperance Union. Laws were later adopted in Massachusetts and Vermont.

In 1853 Ephraim Wales Bull of Concord, MA exhibited Concord Grapes to the Massachusetts Horticultural Society. Within ten years the grapes would be used to produce wine and port.

On 1856 over 200 women with hatchets destroyed every container of alcohol found in Rockport, MA. Even today the town remains dry!!!

In 1844 Harvey P. Hood moved from Vermont to Boston to drive a bakery route in Charlestown for $12 per month. With his savings he bought a farm in Derry, NH to produce milk and founded the Hood Dairy. In 1890 H.P. Hood began retail distribution of his dairy products and began pasteurizing milk in 1896. Glass bottles were first used by the company in 1897.

1851 Herman Melville and eleven others climbed to the top of Mount Greylock, MA. With them they brought brandied fruit, champagne, port, cognac, Jamaican rum, and other supplies to get them through the night. Melville lived at "Arrowhead" in Pittsfield while writing *Moby Dick.* He was introduced to Nathaniel Hawthorne in 1850 by Judge Oliver Wendell Holmes when they climbed Monument Mountain during a storm. At the top they drank a toast to William Cullen Bryant with Heidsieck Champagne.

Case and Sanborn of Boston was the first company to pack roasted coffee in sealed cans in 1878. In 1863 Caleb Chase and James S. Sanborn began selling coffee in Boston.

In 1886 Augustin Thompson of Lowell, MA introduced Moxie Nerve Food, a beverage with sparkling water and gentian root.

The Seaman's Bethel on Martha's Vineyard opened in 1892 as a refuge and chapel away from life's temptations for a sailor or whaler such as drinking or street life.

In 1901 H. Earle Kimball of Boston began selling Clicquot Club Ginger Ale. The ginger ale was named for the French champagne.

Salada Tea was introduced to New York in 1902 and a plant later built in Boston.

In 1908 Hugh Moore invented a vending machine to sell water for a penny a cup in individual cups. In 1909 would be sold under the name Dixie Cups.

In 1910 the world's first glass-lined milk car was put into service on the Boston & Maine Railroad for the Whiting Milk Company.

In 1934 Fred Pabst of the Pabst Brewing Company chose Manchester, VT for a ski resort. In 1936 he bought seventeen acres that would be developed into Bromley Mountain ski resort.

In 1939 G. F. Heublein & Bro., Hartford, CT obtained the rights to Smirnoff vodka for $14,000.

In 1945 Ruth Bigelow, a New York interior decorator, David Bigelow and Bertha Nealey introduced Constant Comment Tea. The company is still located in Norwalk, CT.

The Lyman Estate in Waltham, MA was built by Boston merchant Theodore Lyman. The grounds have elegant gardens and a greenhouse with grape vines from Hampton Court in England.

The Isaac Royall House in Medford, MA was built in 1732. Mr. Royall owned a sugar plantation in Antigua and was part of the Triangular

Trade in rum and slaves. The only surviving slave quarters in Massachusetts are located on the grounds.

Theodore Geisel (Dr. Seuss) grew up in Springfield, MA where his family ran a brewery. During Prohibition the brewery was closed, and his father managed Forest Park and the Springfield Zoo.

CAPE CODDER

Serves 1

1½ ounces vodka   Slice of lime
5 ounces cranberry juice

- ◆ Pour the vodka and cranberry juice over ice in a tall glass. Serve with a slice of lime.

CRANBERRY PUNCH

12 cups cranberry juice   ½ teaspoon allspice
1 cup orange juice   2 cups brandy
¼ cup lemon juice   1 cup bourbon
4 sticks cinnamon

- ◆ Heat the ingredients in a large pot. Pour into a punch bowl. Serve in punch cups.
- ◆ Can also be served without heating in a punch bowl.

SANGRIA

Madeira, rum and wine drinks were popular among the early colonists. Sangria was from the Spanish "sangaree" and was made with red wine, water, sugar, juices and spices.

5 bottles dry red wine	1 lemon, sliced
1 cup brandy	1 lime, sliced
1 bottle club soda	1 orange sliced
½ cup sugar	Ice mold

- In a punch bowl combine the wine, brandy, club soda and sugar.
- Add the ice mold and float the lemon, lime and range slices on top.
- Serve in wine glasses or punch cups.

BACCARDI COCKTAIL

12 glasses

1 bottle dark rum	¼ cup grenadine
1 cup lime juice	2 Tbls. sugar

- Put into a large shaker and shake well.
- Serve over ice with a lime slice and a sprig of mint.

CIDER PUNCH

Makes 24 cups

1 bottle bourbon	Ice mold
½ cup rum	1 apple, thinly sliced
½ gallon cider	1 lemon, thinly sliced
1 bottle ginger ale	

- In a punch combine the bourbon, rum, cider and ginger ale. Place the ice mold in the bowl. Garnish with apple and lemon.

HOT BUTTERED RUM

Perfect for a cold winter's night or after skiing!

4 sticks cinnamon
¼ cup sugar
1 lemon, sliced

½ stick butter
1 bottle dark rum

♦ Heat the ingredients in a sauce pan. Serve in mugs.

STRAWBERRY PEACH DAIQUIRI

Serves 1

1 peach, peeled and pitted
½ cup strawberries
1 Tbls. lime juice

1 teaspoon sugar
1½ oz. dark rum
4 cubes ice

♦ Place all ingredients in blender. Serve in a glass.

MIMOSA

This is a favorite on Sunday morning.

½ part champagne
½ part orange juice

♦ Pour orange juice into a champagne flute and add champagne.
♦ Garnish with a mint leaf and strawberry

SOUPS

The author's daughter, nieces and nephews on the beach at Nantucket

CHAMPAGNE LOBSTER SOUP

Serves 6-8

½ stick butter
3 cups corn
2 leeks, chopped
3 large red bliss potatoes, diced
3 cloves garlic, minced
3 cups milk

3 cups cream
2 pounds lobster meat
1 cup champagne
Salt and pepper to taste
Parsley or basil leaves

- ◆ Melt the butter in a large pot. Add the corn, leeks and potatoes and cook until just tender.
- ◆ Add the garlic, milk and cream. Simmer for 20 minutes. Season with salt and pepper.
- ◆ Just before serving add the lobster, champagne, salt and pepper.
- ◆ Serve in individual bowls or a soup tureen. Garnish with parsley or basil.
- ◆ Crab can be substituted for the lobster.

LOBSTER BISQUE

Serves 4

½ stick butter
½ cup leeks or green onions, chopped
1 stalk celery, chopped
2 Tbls. tomato paste
¼ cup flour

2 cups half and half
2 cups cream
¼ cup Sherry
1 pound lobster meat
Paprika
Basil

- ◆ In a sauce pan melt butter. Add leeks, celery and tomato paste. Stir in flour. Slowly add half and half, then cream, until just thickened.
- ◆ This can be pureed in a food processor or left as is.
- ◆ Add Sherry and lobster meat.
- ◆ Serve in bowls garnished with paprika and basil.
- ◆ If not pureed can be used as Newburg sauce over rice, pasta or in puff pastry

LOBSTER VICHYSSOISE

Serves 8

4 large potatoes, peeled and diced
8 cups chicken stock
1 cup leeks, sliced
2 bunches watercress, chopped

1 cup heavy cream
½ cup white wine
2 pounds lobster meat
Salt and pepper
Chives or parsley

♦ In a large pot heat the potatoes, stock and leeks. Bring to boil and then simmer until potatoes are just softened.
♦ Put in food processor.
♦ Pour back into pot and add other ingredients, except chives.
♦ Serve in bowls with chives or parsley.
♦ Serve hot or chilled

SEAFOOD BISQUE

Serves 4

½ stick butter
1 cup leeks, chopped
1 stalk celery, chopped
2 tomatoes, chopped
¼ cup flour
2 cups cream

¼ cup Sherry
1 teaspoon Worcestershire sauce
½ teaspoon cayenne
½ pound shrimp
½ pound bay scallops
½ pound crab meat or lobster

♦ In a sauce pan melt butter. Add leeks, celery and tomatoes. Stir in flour. Slowly add cream, until just thickened.
♦ This can be pureed in a food processor or left as is.
♦ Add rest of ingredients.
♦ Serve in bowls.
♦ If not pureed can be used as Newburg sauce over rice, pasta or in puff pastry

SEAFOOD CHOWDER

Serves 8

¼ cup olive oil
¼ cup sherry
1 onion, chopped
2 carrots, sliced
2 stalks celery, diced
4 medium red bliss potatoes, chopped

1 tomato, chopped
¼ teaspoon cayenne
6 cups half and half
1 pound shrimp,
1 pound scallops
1 dozen clams
1 dozen mussels

- ◆ In a large pot heat the oil and sherry. Add the onions, carrots, celery, and potatoes and cook until just tender. Add tomatoes, cayenne, half and half. Bring to boil.
- ◆ Add seafood. Season with salt and pepper.
- ◆ Serve warm with crusty bread.

CLAM CHOWDER

Serves 6

6 slices smoked bacon
½ stick butter
6 medium red bliss potatoes, diced
1 small onion, diced
1 stalk celery, diced
1 carrot, sliced

1 cup peas
½ red bell pepper, diced
36 quahaugs
2 quarts half and half
1 teaspoon fresh ground pepper
1 Tbls. fresh tarragon or thyme

- ◆ Preheat oven to 350°.
- ◆ Place clams on a cookie sheet and place in oven until clams just open. Save clam broth.
- ◆ In a pan with water just covering the potatoes, cook potatoes until tender.
- ◆ In a large pot cook the bacon until crisp. Save bacon drippings in pot. Remove bacon. Melt butter. Add potatoes, onion, celery, carrots, and peas. Stir in clam broth.
- ◆ Add half and half, pepper and tarragon. Then clams.
- ◆ Serve in bowls.

MUSSEL SOUP

Serves 6

1 large onion, chopped
3 stalks celery, chopped
½ cup green pepper, chopped
½ cup red pepper, chopped
¼ cup olive oil
3 cups dry white wine
1 teaspoon thyme
2 Tbls. basil, chopped

¼ cup parsley, chopped
2 bay leaves
½ teaspoon sea salt
1 teaspoon fresh ground pepper
3 cloves garlic, minced
3 tomatoes, chopped
6 dozen mussels
1 dozen little neck clams

- ◆ Heat the olive oil in a large pot. Add the onions, celery, and pepper, and sauté until just tender.
- ◆ Add the wine, herbs and tomatoes. Bring to a boil and simmer for 15 minutes.
- ◆ Rinse the mussels and clams. Add them to wine broth. Bring to boil and all shells are opened.
- ◆ Serve immediately with crusty bread.

CRAB & VEGETABLE CHOWDER

Serves 4

2 Tbls. olive oil
¼ cup flour
1 small onion, chopped
½ cup red bell pepper, chopped
½ cup yellow pepper, chopped
1 large carrot, peeled and chopped

2 green onions, chopped
1 stalk celery, chopped
4 large tomatoes, chopped
2 cups chicken broth
1 pound fresh crab meat

- ◆ Combine oil and flour in pot. Stir until a brown roux is formed.
- ◆ Add vegetables.
- ◆ Stir in chicken broth.
- ◆ Just before serving add crab.
- ◆ Serve in bowls or over rice.

VEGETABLE SOUP

Serves 12 or more

2 Tbls. butter
1 large onion, chopped
4 large tomatoes
3 quarts water
4 large carrots, peeled and sliced
2 large potatoes, peeled and diced
1 leek, diced
½ pound string beans

1 15 oz. can kidney beans
3 stalks celery, chopped
2 cups fresh corn
4 cloves garlic, minced
¼ cup basil, chopped
¼ cup parsley, chopped
2 green chilies, seeded and chopped
½ teaspoon cayenne

- In a large pot melt the butter. Stir in onions. Add other ingredients. Bring to a boil. Reduce heat and simmer for 1 hour.
- Serve with crusty bread.

PEA SOUP

Serves 6

4 cups fresh peas
6 cups chicken stock
½ stick butter
¼ cup flour

¼ cup chives, snipped
1 cup heavy cream
1 Tbls. fresh tarragon
½ teaspoon cayenne

- In a sauce pan bring the peas and 2 cups stock to boil. Remove from heat and pour into a bowl.
- In same sauce pan melt butter and add flour and stock. Stir until just slightly thickened. Stir in other ingredients.
- Serve in bowls with a dollop of sour cream and snipped chives.
- Asparagus or mushrooms can be substituted for the peas.

SQUASH SOUP

Serves 4

½ stick butter
2 carrots, peeled and sliced
1 onion, chopped
¼ cup flour
2 cups chicken stock
2 yellow squash, diced

1 cup cheddar cheese
2 cups heavy cream
1 Tbls. curry
Salt and pepper
Cilantro

- Melt the butter in a large pot. Add carrots and onion. Cook until onion is transparent.
- Stir in flour and chicken stock. Add squash and cheese. Cook for 5 minutes or until cheese is just melted.
- Add cream, curry and salt and pepper to taste.
- Serve warm or chilled.
- Serve in bowls. Garnish with cilantro.
- Shrimp, crab or lobster can be added for a hearty meal.

SPICED SQUASH SOUP

Serves 4

½ stick butter, melted
1 medium onion, chopped
1 large butternut squash
1 large acorn squash
2 carrots, sliced

1 quart chicken stock
1 cup apple cider
1 teaspoon cinnamon
2 Tbls. fresh grated ginger

- Preheat oven to 350°
- Cut the squash in half lengthwise and remove seeds. Place on cookie sheet skin side down. Arrange carrots and onions around squash. Sprinkle with butter.
- Bake until squash is just tender.
- Remove from oven. Take skin off squash. Dice squash.
- In a large pot combine all ingredients. Bring to a boil.
- Serve hot in bowls.

PUMPKIN SOUP

Serves 4

½ stick butter
1 small onion, chopped
2 green onions, chopped
1 15 oz. canned pumpkin

2 cups chicken broth
2 cups cream
2 teaspoons cinnamon
1 cup toasted pumpkin seed

- ◆ Preheat oven to 350°
- ◆ Place the pumpkin seeds on a cookie sheet. Bake for 10 minutes or until just toasted.
- ◆ Melt the butter in a large pot. Add onions. Add pumpkin. Cook for five minutes. Stir in chicken broth.
- ◆ Just before serving add cream and cinnamon.
- ◆ Serve in bowls and garnish with pumpkin seeds.

CURRIED ZUCCHINI SOUP

Serves 6

½ stick butter
1 medium onion, chopped
1 celery stalk, chopped
2 cloves garlic, minced
1 Tbls. curry or more
3 zucchini, peeled and diced
1 teaspoon salt

3 cups chicken stock
2 Tbls. lemon juice
2 cups heavy cream
¼ cup dark rum
Fresh dill can be substituted for the rum

- ◆ Melt the butter in a pot. Add onions until transparent. Add celery and garlic.
- ◆ Stir in curry, zucchini, salt, stock and lemon juice.
- ◆ Just before serving stir in cream and rum.
- ◆ Serve warm or chilled with snipped fresh dill.

ASPARAGUS AND TOMATO SOUP

Serves 6

½ stick butter
4 green onions, chopped
2 teaspoons curry powder
¼ cup flour
6 cups chicken broth
2 medium red bliss potatoes, peeled and diced

1 large tomato, chopped finally
1 pound asparagus, cut into 1 inch lengths. Save tips.
1 cup sour cream
¼ cup fresh dill, snipped

- Melt the butter in a sauce pan. Add onions and curry. Stir in flour and chicken broth.
- Add potatoes. Cook for 15-20 minutes, or until potatoes are tender.
- Stir in tomatoes and asparagus.
- Place mixture in food processor and puree.
- Stir in sour cream.
- Serve in bowls and garnished with asparagus tips and dill.
- Serve warm or chilled.

TOMATO SOUP

Serves 6

6 large tomatoes
2 medium onions, chopped
½ stick butter
2 cups chicken stock
½ cup heavy cream

Salt and pepper to taste
¼ cup fresh basil, chopped
2 avocados, peeled, pitted and sliced

- In a large sauce pan bring water to boil. Drop in the tomatoes for 4 minutes. Remove tomatoes. Peel and finely chop the tomatoes.
- Empty the water from the pan.
- Melt the butter in the pan. Add the onions and saute until transparent. Add the tomatoes. Stir in the chicken stock and then the cream. Add salt and pepper.
- The basil can be added to the soup or sprinkled on top. Serve warm or chilled with avocado slices.
- Dill can be substituted for the basil.

TOMATO LEEK SOUP

Serves 6

½ stick butter
2 leeks, chopped
2 large carrots, sliced
8 plum tomatoes, chopped
2 cups tomato juice

4 cups chicken broth
Salt and pepper to taste
¼ cup fresh basil leaves
Croutons
Sour cream

- In a large sauce pan melt the butter and sauté the leeks and carrots until just tender. Add the tomatoes, tomato juice and chicken broth. Bring to a boil. Turn down heat and simmer for 20 minutes. Season with salt and pepper.
- Puree in a food processor.
- Serve in bowls with the basil, some croutons and a dab of sour cream.

WATERCRESS SOUP

Serves 6

½ stick butter
3 large leeks, chopped
2 bunches watercress, stems removed

4 cups chicken broth
2 cups heavy cream
1 teaspoon fresh ground pepper
Toasted sliced almonds

- In a large sauce pan melt the butter. Sautee the leeks until just tender about 7 minutes. Stir in the watercress and add the stock.
- Place in a food processor and puree.
- Add the cream and pepper.
- Pour into soup bowls and garnish with the almonds.

CARROT SOUP

Serves 6

½ stick butter
1 large onion, chopped
3 cloves garlic, crushed
1 ½ pounds carrots, chopped
4 cups chicken broth
3 Tbls. fresh basil

3 Tbls. fresh parsley, chopped
1 teaspoon kosher salt
1 teaspoon fresh ground pepper
2 cups heavy cream
Fresh basil and parsley leaves
Sour cream

♦ In a large sauce pan melt the butter and stir in the onion and garlic until transparent. Stir in carrots, chicken broth, basil, parsley, salt and pepper. Bring to a boil and cook until the carrots are tender, about ½ hour.
♦ Remove from heat and place in food processor until smooth. Fold in cream.
♦ Serve in bowls garnished with basil and parsley leaves and a dollop of sour cream.

BEAN SOUP

Serves 6

4 slices bacon, diced
1 medium onion, chopped
2 cloves garlic, minced
2 bay leaves

2 15 oz. cans black beans
6 cups chicken broth
2 Tbls. fresh rosemary
Salt and pepper to taste

♦ In a large pot cook the bacon until crisp. Add the onion and garlic, stirring until translucent. Reduce the heat and add the beans, bay leaves, chicken broth, rosemary, salt and pepper. Cook for 20 minutes.
♦ Remove bay leaves and puree in food processor.
♦ Serve in individual bowls with a dollop of sour cream and rosemary.

CORN CHOWDER

Serves 4

3 slices bacon
1 medium onion, peeled and chopped
3 cups fresh corn
2 cups wild rice
4 cups chicken broth

1 stalk celery, chopped
1 pound smoked turkey, cubed
1 teaspoon marjoram
½ teaspoon paprika
Salt and pepper

- ◆ In a large pot sauté the bacon slices. Add the onion and sauté.
- ◆ Add the other ingredients. Bring to a boil.
- ◆ Simmer for 30 minutes or until rice is tender.
- ◆ Serve in bowls garnished with chopped scallions.
- ◆ 2 cups diced cooked chicken or crab meat can be substituted for the turkey. Serve with a salad and crusty bread.

BLUEBERRY SOUP

Serves 4

2 cups blueberries
½ lemon, sliced
2 sticks cinnamon
2 cups water

¼ cup orange juice
1 Tbls. cornstarch
Mint leaves
Lemon slices

- ◆ In a sauce pan bring the blueberries, lemon slices, cinnamon and water to a boil and simmer 10 minutes.
- ◆ Add orange juice and cornstarch. Bring to a boil. Remove cinnamon. Puree in food processor. Cool.
- ◆ Serve in bowls and garnish with mint leaves and lemon slices.

COLD CURRIED APPLE SOUP

Serves 8

2 medium onions, peeled and chopped
2 cups celery, chopped
2 apples, peeled and cored
1 stick butter
2 Tbls. flour

6 cups chicken broth
2 cups heavy cream
1 Tbls. curry
Croutons
Sliced apples

- ◆ In a large pot melt the butter and sauté the onions, celery and apples. Remove from heat.
- ◆ Place in a food processor until pureed.
- ◆ In a sauce pan combine puree and stock. Bring to a boil.
- ◆ Place in a bowl and chill.
- ◆ Add cream and curry just before serving.
- ◆ More curry can be added. Serve with croutons and sliced apples.

HAM SOUP

Serves

4 cups water
2 chicken bouillon cubes
1 large ham hock with at least a half pound of ham meat left
½ teaspoon nutmeg
1 teaspoon cinnamon
1 15 oz. can black beans, drained

1 15 oz. can red kidney beans, drained
1 medium onion chopped
2 large tomatoes, chopped
½ teaspoon thyme
½ teaspoon cayenne
A couple drops hot sauce
½ cup dark rum

- ◆ In a large pot combine the water, bouillon cubes, ham hock, nutmeg, cinnamon, beans and onion.
- ◆ Cook at least 1 hour, or until ham falls off bone.
- ◆ Add tomatoes, thyme, cayenne and hot sauce. Add more if needed.
- ◆ Stir in rum just before serving, or serve in a separate pitcher.

SEAFOOD

A scuttlebutt was a water cask on a ship, around which sailors would congregate and exchange the "latest gossip" or "scuttlebutt".

Every August the author and Tom Bispham celebrate their birthday with a lobster feast at the Barnacle. In the picture are George Moose, the author's husband, the author, Barbara and Tom Bispham, and the author's parents.

John Smith explored the Maine coast in 1614 and commented on the abundance of "lobsters...fruits, birds, crabs...and such excellent fish as many as their net can hold". Boothbay Harbor he decided was an "ideal" fishing station. The Isles of Shoals were originally called Smith's Islands and were inhabited by male fishermen only until 1647 when one man asked the General Court of Massachusetts if he could bring his wife with him.

By 1639 cod fishing had become such an economically viable commodity to New England that the fishermen were exempt from military duty and fishing gear was declared free from taxes. In 1640 the Massachusetts Bay Colony shipped over 300,000 codfish. By 1700 Boston was shipping over 50,000 quintals of dried codfish to such places as Bilbao, Oporto and Lisbon, Portugal in exchange for Port. Dried cod was once sent from New England to the West Indies to feed the slaves on the plantations. In exchange for dried fish, flour, and barrels Boston and Providence and the other cities imported wine, sugar, molasses.

In 1784 John Rowe proposed to the Massachusetts House of Representatives that "a representation of a cod fish" be hung in the room where the House meets to symbolize the importance of the codfish industry in the Commonwealth. The 4'11" model was called "The Sacred Cod". A codfish still hangs in the State House in Boston.

Gorton's fish factory was founded in 1755 in Gloucester, MA. In 1846 William Underwood of Boston began packing fish and shellfish in Maine. The oldest printed recipe for fish chowder appeared in the Boston Evening Post on September 23, 1751. Farmhouse chowders originated on the islands (Nantucket and Martha's Vineyard) using local products such as fish, beans and corn. In 1955 they moved into a $1.5 million facility and began producing frozen fish sticks and frozen fish dinners, in addition to codfish cakes. Wesley George Pierce was born in Gloucester in 1869, spending time as a fisherman and wrote *Goin' Fishin'*. In 1916 *The Tattler*, the largest two-masted fishing schooner out of Gloucester, set a record by landing half a million pounds of cod on one trip. In 1895 a 211.5 pound cod was caught by Massachusetts fishermen using a line trawl. By 1993 the U.S. cod catch had fallen to 49 million pounds, the lowest since 1973.

New Bedford was once a farming community settled by Quakers from Rhode Island and Cape Cod. The city realized the importance of its harbor in the 1760s and in 1765 Joseph Russell sent his first whaling ships to sea. As whale oil gave way to oil, New Bedford's fishing fleet grew, though in the 1970s declined. New Bedford still relies on its catch of haddock, cod and scallops. The *Ernestina*, a training vessel in New Bedford is an 1894 Gloucester fishing schooner.

The waters off Truro on Cape Cod were considered extremely treacherous and in 1797 Truro was chosen by the federal government as the site of the first lighthouse on Cape Cod. During a storm in 1841 fifty-seven Truro fishermen lost their lives. The Museum of the Truro Historical Society is located in a former inn, and maintains a collection of items lost in some of these shipwrecks. Wellfleet was known for its oysters as early as 1606. Samuel de Champlain explored the area and named the harbor "Oyster Port". Later whaling became important to the town.

Around Lake Sunapee, New Hampshire "wild goose water" many farms prospered, but the climate was not predictable. In 1821 a tornado roared through the area that was immortalized in Charles Dickens short story *The Fishermen of Sunapee.*

In 1889 the Maine salmon catch was 150,000 pounds. By 1950 only 82 Atlantic salmon were caught off the coast of Maine. In 1990 Maine lobstermen caught 28 million pounds of lobster. The last record was in 1889 with 24 million pounds. The largest lobster fleets in Downeast Maine are maintained in Jonesport and Beals Island.

South Norwalk, CT was once the oyster capital of the Northeast. The Matabesecs tribe taught the first settlers how to seed oyster beds. Captain Peter Decker invented the steam-powered dredge in 1874.

Essex, MA has tidal flats that are noted for their clams. Woodman's of Essex claims that "Chubby" Woodman invented the fried clam here over eighty years ago. Essex still holds a clamfest in mid-September.

Eastport, ME once had eighteen sardine canneries. Julius Wolfe invented the canning machinery in 1785. However, the sardine business died out in the 1970s. Now the town is one of the largest producers of farmed Atlantic salmon in North America.

Clarence Birdseye founded General Seafoods in Gloucester, MA in 1924. In 1925 they began selling quick frozen fish fillets.

In 1950 George Berkowitz opened a fish market in Cambridge, MA next to the Legal Cash Market, later becoming Legal Seafoods.

New England is noted not only for seafood but for fresh water fish also. Brown and brook trout from the Brewster River; wild trout, walleyed pike and salmon from Lake Memphremagog; trout and salmon from Lake Willoughby, all in Vermont. The Rangeley Lakes, Moosehead Lake, Penobscot, Allagash and Moose Rivers in Maine are well stocked with landlocked salmon and brook trout.

Charles Orvis, the father of fly fishing in America lived in Manchester, VT. The American Museum of Fly Fishing and the Orvis Company are located in Manchester.

Lobsters shed their shells annually, with the molt taking place in July and August. New shells grow back, but during the time period July to September, lobsters can be watery. The best time for eating them is during the winter. Lobstering became a profitable Maine industry in the 1840s. However, they were in such abundance that they often were thought of as poor people's food.

LOBSTER IN PUFF PASTRY

Serves 6

Puff pastry	2 cups corn
1½ pounds lobster	Cherry tomatoes
1 pound asparagus, cut into 1"	Grated fresh parmesan cheese
pieces	Fresh basil leaves

- ♦ Preheat oven to 425°
- ♦ Roll the pastry into 6 squares about ¼" thick.
- ♦ Divide the lobster, asparagus, corn and ½ basil butter among the pastries. Fold over edges and seal with water.
- ♦ Bake for 25 minutes or until just browned.

Basil Butter

1 stick butter, softened	2 Tbls. parsley, chopped
½ cup basil leaves, chopped	2 Tbls. lemon juice

- ♦ Combine all ingredients in a food processor until smooth.
- ♦ Spoon rest on each pastry just before serving. Garnish with cherry tomatoes and fresh basil leaves.

LOBSTER THERMIDOR

Serves 6

6 1½ pound lobsters

- ♦ Bring 2 inches of water to a boil in a large pot. Add the lobsters and cover with a lid. Cook for 15 minutes. Remove lobsters with tongs. Save stock. Remove the claws and crack the claw to loosen the meat. Remove the meat from the tails and save tails.

Bechamel Sauce

1 stick unsalted butter
1 cup leek, diced
1 carrot, peeled and sliced
1 stalk celery, diced
½ red pepper, chopped
½ yellow pepper, chopped
½ pound mushrooms
½ cup flour
2 cups heavy cream

2 egg yolks
½ teaspoon salt
1 teaspoon fresh ground pepper
¼ teaspoon nutmeg
Pinch of cayenne
1 Tbls. chopped fresh tarragon
¼ cup brandy
½ cup grated parmesan cheese

- ♦ Preheat oven to 425 degrees.
- ♦ Melt butter in a saucepan and saute leek, carrot and celery until translucent. Add pepper and mushrooms. Add flour and cream, stirring until thickened. Add egg yolks.
- ♦ Remove from heat. Stir in rest of ingredients, except cheese.
- ♦ Chop the lobster meat. Add to ½ the cream mixture.
- ♦ Place the tails in a casserole. Place lobster mixture on each tail. Top with more sauce and grated cheese.
- ♦ Bake for 12 minutes or until just browned and bubbling.

NEW ENGLAND CLAMBAKE

Clambakes are a traditional pastime of the summer. Though not as frequent as they used to be every New England family has memories of how they sat around the fire, and awaited the moment when the seaweed was removed and the eating could begin.

The basic ingredients for a clambake are lobster, clams, corn on the cob, and potatoes. Add to this a salad, Portuguese bread, butter, salt and pepper, followed by watermelon and fruit. One can never feel underfed. Start early in the afternoon on preparation.

THE CLAMBAKE

Serves 12

24 ears of corn
12 1½ pound lobsters
12 large baking potatoes

6 dozen clams in shell
Melted butter
Lemons

- Most places you do need a permit for a fire, so make sure this is in hand, before finding the perfect beach site for your gathering.
- Dig a large hole in the sand and line with any rocks you can find on the beach.
- Add driftwood and hardwood charcoal. Start a fire.
- Walk along the beach and gather seaweed.
- After an hour or two the rocks will get quite hot. Cover them with some of the seaweed. Place the lobsters on top. Cover with more seaweed. Add the clams. Add more seaweed, then foil covered potatoes, and corn in their husks.
- Cover with a tarpaulin weighted down with stones. Bake for 1 hour. Make sure the clams have opened their shells.
- Serve immediately.

STEAMED MUSSELS

Serves 4

48 mussels, scrubbed
4 shallots, chopped
4 cloves garlic, chopped

4 tomatoes, chopped
¼ cup basil, chopped
1 cup white wine

- ♦ Place all the ingredients in a large pot. Bring to a boil and mussels open. Discard any unopened mussels.
- ♦ Serve with crusty bread or pasta and a salad.

CURRIED MUSSELS

Serves 6

1 cup white wine
4 dozen mussels
3 scallions, chopped
3 cloves garlic, crushed

1 Tbls. curry
2 cups cooked rice
3 Tbls. fresh ginger, grated

- ♦ In a large pot heat the white wine, mussels, scallions and garlic until the mussels open. Remove from heat and discard any mussels that did not open. Save the liquor.
- ♦ Remove one shell from the mussels and the mussel. In the pot combine the mussels, rice, ginger and liquor.
- ♦ Spoon the mixture into the mussel shells.
- ♦ Serve hot with a salad and crusty bread.

MUSSEL FRITTERS

Serves 6-8

1 cup water
4 dozen mussels
1 whole shallot, chopped
2 bay leaves, crushed
¼ cup fresh parsley, chopped
½ cup white wine

1 cup cream
1 egg
1½ cups flour
1 teaspoon baking powder
Vegetable oil

- In a large pot bring the water and mussels to a boil and the shells open. Discard any mussels that do not open. Chop mussels.
- In a bowl combine the shallot, bay leaves, parsley, wine, cream, egg, flour, baking powder and mussels to make a batter. If too runny add more flour.
- Drop into a skillet with hot vegetable oil. Fry until just crispy. Drain on paper towels.
- Serve with cold slaw or horseradish sauce.
- These can also be served as an hors d'oeuvres.
- A variation on this is to leave the mussels whole. Dip them in batter and fry.
- Clams can be substituted for the mussels.

MUSSELS AND CHORIZO

Serves 6

4 dozen mussels
1 cup white wine
1 pound chorizo, cubed

3 medium tomatoes, finely chopped
3 cloves garlic, minced

- Place all the ingredients in a large pot. Bring to a boil. Simmer for 5 minutes.
- Serve with crusty bread or over rice.

MUSSELS IMPERIAL

Serves 6 as an entree

4 dozen mussels   2 cups white wine

♦ Cook mussels in wine until shells open. Discard any mussels that do not open. Remove shells and save mussels.

Crab Imperial

2 pounds crab meat   2 eggs
1 teaspoon Dijon mustard   Juice of 1 lemon
1 cup mayonnaise   1 tsp. Worcestershire sauce
1 teaspoon salt   ¼ teaspoon cayenne
1 green pepper, chopped   ¼ teaspoon pepper

♦ Preheat oven to 350°.
♦ Combine all the ingredients in a bowl except for the crab.
♦ Place six mussels in individual ramekins. Top with crab meat. Spoon the mayonnaise mixture on top.
♦ Bake for 15 minutes or until bubbling and just browned.
♦ Sprinkle with paprika before serving.
♦ Serve with rice or crusty bread and a salad.

SCALLOPS WITH CITRUS VINAIGRETTE

Serves 4

2 pounds sea scallops   ¼ cup olive oil
¼ cup lime juice   ¼ cup mint, chopped
2 Tbls. grated ginger   2 Tbls. Cointreau

♦ Combine all ingredients in a bowl.
♦ Serve as an entrée or appetizer.

SCALLOPS IN LOBSTER SAUCE

Serves 4

2 pounds sea scallops   1 pint cherry tomatoes
¼ cup olive oil   ¼ cup basil

- ◆ Saute the scallops in olive oil. Place on platter and garnish with lobster sauce, cherry tomatoes and basil.

Lobster Brandy Sauce

½ stick butter   ¼ cup brandy
¼ cup flour   1 pound lobster meat
1 cup cream

- ◆ Melt butter in sauce pan. Stir in flour and cream. Add brandy and lobster.

SEAFOOD WITH LOBSTER SAUCE

Serves 8

2 pounds sea scallops (without   1 pound crab meat
shells)   Puff pastry
2 pounds shrimp, cooked, peeled
and deveined

- ◆ Grill the scallops and shrimp on a BBG.
- ◆ Combine scallops, shrimp and crab in a bowl.
- ◆ Place seafood in puff pastry and top with lobster sauce.

Lobster Sauce

1 stick butter
¼ cup flour   ½ cup Sherry
1½ cups heavy cream   1 pound lobster meat

- ◆ Melt the butter in a sauce pan.
- ◆ Add the flour and stir in the cream and Sherry until thickened.
- ◆ Fold in the lobster.

SCALLOPS WITH DILL SAUCE

Serves 4

2 pounds sea scallops

- ♦ Grill scallops on BBQ. Serve on a platter with dill sauce.

Dill Hollandaise Sauce

¼ cup lemon juice   1 stick butter, melted
2 Tbls. tarragon vinegar   ¼ cup fresh dill
3 egg yolks

- ♦ Combine all ingredients in food processor until thickened.

COQUILLES

Serves 4

1½ pounds bay scallops   ½ cup flour
½ pound mushrooms, sliced   ¼ pound Gruyere
1 Tbls. shallot, chopped   Salt and pepper to taste
1 cup dry white wine   ¼ teaspoon cayenne
1 stick butter   ½ cup bread crumbs
1½ cups cream

- ♦ Preheat broiler.
- ♦ In a skillet melt 2 Tbls. butter. Add the mushrooms and saute for 3 minutes.
- ♦ Add the scallops, shallots and wine, and cook for 5 minutes.
- ♦ Add the cream and bring to a boil. Season with salt, pepper, and cayenne.
- ♦ In a saucepan melt the remaining butter and stir in flour. Pour this into the scallop mixture and add Gruyere. Cook for 2 minutes. When this has thickened pour the mixture into 6 large scallop shells. Top with bread crumbs.
- ♦ Place under broiler until just browned.
- ♦ Serve on fish plates and garnish with parsley.

BAKED SCALLOPS

Serves 4

½ stick butter
½ cup flour
1½ cups heavy cream
¼ cup dry white wine
1 pound asparagus, sliced in 2"
pieces

½ pound mushrooms, sliced
2 cloves garlic, minced
2 green onions, chopped
¼ cup fresh basil, chopped
2 pounds sea scallops

- ♦ Preheat oven to 350°
- ♦ Melt the butter in a sauce pan. Stir in flour, cream and wine.
- ♦ In a greased baking dish combine all ingredients.
- ♦ Bake 20 minutes or until bubbling and just browned.
- ♦ Serve with rice or pasta

BAKED SCALLOPS II

Serves 4

½ stick butter, melted
2 Tbls. parsley, chopped
2 cloves garlic, minced
2 pounds bay scallops

Juice of 1 lemon
¼ cup white wine
¼ cup fresh basil
1½ cups dry bread crumbs

- ♦ Preheat oven to 350°
- ♦ Combine all ingredients in a greased baking dish.
- ♦ Bake 20 minutes, or until just browned and bubbling.
- ♦ Serve with rice.

BAKED SCALLOPS III

Serves 6

½ cup shallots, chopped
½ stick butter, melted
¼ cup lime juice
¼ teaspoon cayenne
½ teaspoon salt

1 teaspoon fresh ground pepper
2 ½ pounds sea scallops
1 cup leeks, chopped
1 pound porcini mushrooms, sliced

- ◆ Preheat oven to 350°
- ◆ Combine all ingredients in a greased baking dish.
- ◆ Bake 20 minutes, or until just browned and bubbling.
- ◆ Serve with rice.

SAUTEED SCALLOPS AND SHRIMP

Serves 6

2 Tbls. olive oil
3 tomatoes, chopped
½ red bell pepper, chopped
½ yellow pepper, chopped
½ pound asparagus, cut in 1" pieces
½ pound mushrooms, sliced

3 cloves garlic, minced
3 green onions, chopped
2 ½ pounds bay scallops
1 pound medium shrimp, cooked, peeled and deveined
¼ cup parsley
¼ cup lemon juice

- ◆ Heat the olive oil in a skillet. Stir in vegetables until just tender.
- ◆ Add scallops, shrimp, parsley, and lemon juice.
- ◆ Serve over rice.
- ◆ Basil can be substituted for parsley.

STIR-FRIED SCALLOPS

Serves 6

1½ pounds sea scallops   Juice of 1 lemon
1½ pounds asparagus   2 Tbls. sesame oil
3 cloves garlic, minced   3 Tbls. fresh dill, snipped

- In a bowl combine the scallops, asparagus, garlic and lemon juice.
- Heat oil in a wok. Stir in the scallops and asparagus.
- Garnish with the dill. Serve over rice.

GRILLED SCALLOPS

Serves 8 for a main course with rice, or can be used as an appetizer.
Mussels can be substituted for the scallops.

3 pound fresh sea scallops   ½ pound bacon
Juice of 1 lime   Bearnaise Sauce – p. 206

- In a bowl marinate the scallops in the lime juice for at least 1 hour.
- Wrap the bacon around the scallops.
- Grill the scallops on a grill until just browned.
- Serve scallops on fish platter with bowl of Bearnaise sauce.

SCALLOP AND SHRIMP BROCHETTES

Serves 4

1 pound medium shrimp
1½ pounds sea scallops
1 red bell pepper, cubed
1 yellow pepper cubed
1 large red onion, cubed

¼ cup olive oil
¼ cup white wine
2 Tbls. soy sauce
2 Tbls. fresh grated ginger
2 cloves garlic, minced

- Combine all ingredients in a bowl.
- Alternate shrimp, scallops and vegetables on skewers.
- Grill on BBQ about 2 minutes to a side.

SEAFOOD IN CHARDONNAY SAUCE

Serves 6

1 pound medium shrimp,
cooked, peeled and deveined
1 pound bay scallops
1 pound salmon filets
1 pound tuna filets
¼ cup lemon juice
¼ cup olive oil
¼ cup basil, chopped

1 stick butter
½ cup flour
2 cups heavy cream
1 cup Chardonnay
4 cloves garlic, minced
1 leek, sliced
1 pound wild mushrooms, sliced
Puff pastry shells

- Place the fish in a deep dish and cover with lemon juice and olive oil. Grill fish on BBQ. Cut salmon and tuna into bite size pieces.
- In a saucepan melt the butter, stir in flour and add cream until thickened. Stir in Chardonnay, garlic, leek and mushrooms. Fold in fish.
- Serve in puff pastry.
- This can also be served over linguine or other pasta, or rice.

SEAFOOD NEWBURG

Serves 8

1½ sticks butter
1 pound mushrooms, sliced
¾ cup flour
2 cups cream
½ cup Chardonnay or ¼ cup
Sherry

1 pound shrimp, cooked, peeled
and deveined
1 pound bay scallops
1 pound crab meat
1 pound lobster meat
¼ cup basil, chopped
Puff pastry

- Melt the butter in a large sauce pan. Add flour and stir in cream. Add wine. Stir in seafood and basil.
- Serve in puff pastry or over rice.

MIXED GRILLED SEAFOOD

Serves 6

6 lobster tails
1 pound shrimp, cooked, peeled
and deveined
1 pound Bay scallops

2 dozen mussels
1 pound swordfish, cut in pieces
¼ cup lime juice
¼ cup olive oil

- Place the seafood in a bowl with the lime juice and olive oil. Refrigerate for at least 2 hours.
- Grill on BBQ until just browned and mussels open.
- Place the seafood on a platter or on individual plates.
- Serve herb butter in small bowls to dip seafood in.

Herb Butter Sauce

1 stick butter
¼ cup basil, chopped

2 Tbls. tarragon, snipped
2 Tbls. dill, snipped

- Melt the butter in a sauce pan. Add herbs.

JAMBALAYA

Serves 10

1 pound shrimp, cooked, peeled and deveined
2 dozen mussels
2 dozen scallops
2 dozen clams
1 pound salmon filet, cut into pieces
1 pound swordfish, cut into pieces
½ cup bourbon
2 pounds chorizo
4 slices bacon
1 medium onion, chopped

2 scallions, chopped
1 stalk celery
1 red pepper, chopped
1 green pepper, chopped
4 medium tomatoes, chopped
5 cloves garlic, minced
2 bay leaves
¼ cup parsley, chopped
¼ teaspoon cayenne
1 teaspoon salt
1 teaspoon pepper
2 cups rice
4 cups water

- Combine the seafood and bourbon in a bowl. Marinate for at least 4 hours.
- Preheat oven to 400°
- Place the chorizo in a baking dish and bake for 15 minutes, or until just browned. Remove and cut into pieces.
- Brown the bacon in a pot. Remove bacon and crumble. Sauté the onion, scallions, celery, and peppers until onions are transparent, in the pot using bacon drippings.
- Add other vegetables, seasonings, rice and water.
- Bring to a boil. Reduce heat and cook for 25 minutes.
- Add seafood, bourbon and sausage. Just heat until all ingredients are warm.
- Chicken can be substituted for seafood.

GRILLED TUNA

Serves 6

2½ pounds tuna
Juice of 1 lemon

2 cloves garlic, crushed
2 Tbls. olive oil

- ◆ Combine lemon juice, garlic and olive oil. Place tuna in a dish and cover with mixture. Cover and refrigerate for at least 1 hour.
- ◆ Grill on BBQ to desired doneness.
- ◆ Put on individual plates and serve with basil blueberry succotash

Blueberry, Basil Succotash

2 cups fresh corn, shucked
2 cups fresh lima beans
½ stick butter, melted

1 cup blueberries
½ cup fresh basil leaves

- ◆ In a sauce pan cook corn and lima beans in boiling water until just tender.
- ◆ In a bowl combine the butter, basil and blueberries. Spoon over the beans and corn.

TUNA KEBABS

Serves 6

2½ pounds tuna
Juice of 1 lime
¼ cup soy sauce
2 Tbls. fresh ginger, grated

2 scallions, chopped
1 pound asparagus, cut in 1 inch pieces
Toasted sesame seeds

- ◆ Cut the tuna into 1½ inch cubes.
- ◆ Combine the lime juice, soy sauce and ginger. Marinate the tuna in the lime mixture for at least 4 hours.
- ◆ Place the tuna on kebob sticks. Reserve marinade.
- ◆ Grill on the BBQ until just browned.
- ◆ Blanch the asparagus
- ◆ Combine the marinade with scallions and asparagus.
- ◆ Serve tuna on platter, topped with scallions, asparagus and sesame seeds.

CIOPPINO

Serves 8-10

¼ cup olive oil
1 medium onion, chopped
½ red bell pepper, chopped
½ yellow pepper, chopped
6 large tomatoes, chopped
2 cups dry white wine
¼ cup fresh basil chopped
¼ cup fresh parsley, chopped
3 bay leaves

½ teaspoon cayenne
1 pound large shrimp, cooked, peeled and deveined
2 pound bay scallops
2 pounds tuna, cut into 1 ½ inch pieces
2 dozen mussels
24 quahaugs in shell

- ♦ In a large pot heat the oil. Add the peppers and onion. Cook until onion is transparent. Add tomatoes and white wine.
- ♦ Stir in herbs.
- ♦ Bring to a boil. Simmer for 5 minutes.
- ♦ Add seafood.
- ♦ Serve with crusty bread or rice.

MARINATED SHRIMP

This can be served as a main dish or hors d'oeuvres

Serves 4

1½ pounds large shrimp, cooked, peeled and deveined
¼ cup olive oil
¼ cup white wine
2 large cloves garlic, grated

3 Tbls. parsley
3 Tbls basil
1 teaspoon kosher salt
½ teaspoon fresh ground pepper
Juice of 1 lemon

- ♦ Combine all ingredients in a bowl.
- ♦ Cover and refrigerate for at least four hours.
- ♦ Serve with lemon slices

SEAFOOD CURRY

Serves 8

2 pounds shrimp, cooked, peeled and deveined
2 pounds scallops
2 pounds swordfish, cut into cubes
Juice of two limes
½ stick butter
1 small onion, chopped
2 garlic cloves, minced
2 Tbls. curry powder

4 plum tomatoes, chopped
1 small red pepper, chopped
2 Tbls. fresh ginger, grated
2 jalapeno, seeded and chopped
3 cups fish stock or chicken stock
¼ cup cilantro, chopped
½ teaspoon salt
1 teaspoon fresh ground pepper

- In a bowl combine the shrimp, scallops and swordfish with the lime juice. Let marinate for at least one hour in the refrigerator.
- Place the fish on a baking sheet and broil for just a couple of minutes until tender. The fish is also good grilled.
- In a skillet heat the butter and saute the onion and garlic until translucent. Add the curry powder. Stir in the tomatoes and pepper. Add the ginger, jalapeno fish stock, cilantro, salt and pepper.
- Stir in the seafood. Serve with rice.

SWORDFISH WITH MINT SAUCE

Serves 6

Juice of 1 lemon
Zest of 1 lemon
¼ cup olive oil
2 cloves garlic, crushed
¼ cup fresh mint leaves

½ teaspoon kosher salt
1 teaspoon fresh ground pepper
2 ½ pounds swordfish
¼ cup sour cream
¼ cup mayonnaise

- In a shallow dish combine the lemon juice, lemon zest, olive oil, garlic, ½ of the mint, salt and pepper. Add the swordfish. Cover and refrigerate for at least 2 hours.
- Remove the swordfish, reserving the sauce.
- Combine the remaining sauce with the mayonnaise, sour cream and rest of the mint.
- Grill the swordfish on a barbecue. Place on a platter. Serve the sauce in a bowl with the swordfish.

SWORDFISH WITH GREEN SAUCE

Serves 8

3 pounds swordfish   Juice of 1 lemon

♦ Sprinkle the lemon over the swordfish. Cook on grill.

Green Sauce

1 stick butter   1 whole shallot, peeled and
½ pound mushrooms, sliced   chopped
¼ cup flour   1 cup white wine
1 cup fresh basil leaves,   1 cup heavy cream
chopped

♦ In a sauce pan melt the butter and add the mushrooms and shallots, cooking until just tender.
♦ Stir in the flour and add cream until thickened. Add wine and thicken. Stir in the basil leaves.
♦ Serve in a bowl with the swordfish.

BAKED BLUEFISH

Serves 6

2 ½ pounds bluefish fillets   1 teaspoon salt
¼ cup olive oil   ½ cup fresh parsley, chopped
1 large onion, chopped   1 cup dried cranberries
½ cup pine nuts   3 medium tomatoes, finely
6 slices Portuguese bread, cubed   chopped
1 teaspoon fresh ground pepper   6 slices lemons

♦ Preheat the oven to 350°.
♦ In a skillet heat the olive oil and add the onion, stirring until transparent. Add the nuts, bread, pepper, salt, parsley, cranberries, and tomatoes.
♦ Place the fillets in a baking dish. Cover with the bread mixture.
♦ Bake 30 minutes.
♦ Remove from oven and place on serving platter. Garnish with lemon slices.

BAKED STUFFED BLUEFISH

Serves 6

1 5½ pound bluefish, cleaned, but with head left on

- ♦ Preheat oven to 350°
- ♦ Place the bluefish in a greased baking dish.
- ♦ Stuff the fish with stuffing.
- ♦ Bake 45 minutes or until just browned.
- ♦ Serve on fish platter garnished with parsley and lemon

Stuffing

½ stick butter
1 large tomato, chopped
¼ cup fresh parsley
3 green onions, chopped

2 cups fresh bread cubes
1 Tbls. kosher salt
1 teaspoon fresh ground pepper

- ♦ Melt the butter in a skillet.
- ♦ Add other ingredients and stir until bread is just browned.

EASY BAKED SCROD

Serves 4

2 Tbls. olive oil
1½ pounds scrod filets
Juice of 2 lemons
salt, pepper
¼ cup parsley; chopped

½ pound porcini mushrooms;
chopped
2 scallions; chopped
½ c fresh bread crumbs
½ teaspoon thyme

- ♦ Preheat oven to 350°
- ♦ Place the scrod in a baking dish. Sprinkle the scrod with the lemon juice, salt, pepper and then other ingredients
- ♦ Bake 20 minutes or until just browned.

CLAMS AND CHORIZO

Serves 6

¼ cup olive oil
3 onions, sliced
3 cloves garlic, crushed
Dash of Tabasco
1 teaspoon kosher salt
1 Tbls. fresh ground pepper

3 tomatoes, chopped
1½ pounds chorizo, chopped
½ cup white wine
¼ cup parsley, chopped
48 clams

- ◆ Heat the olive oil in a large pot and onions stirring until transparent. Add the garlic, Tabasco, salt, pepper, tomatoes, chorizo, wine and parsley. Simmer for 10 minutes.
- ◆ Place the clams on top. Cover and simmer for 10 minutes.
- ◆ Serve with rice.

FRIED CLAMS

Serves 6

60 clams, preferably Ipswich
4 eggs, beaten
2 cups Japanese bread crumbs
¼ teaspoon cayenne

Vegetable oil
Lemon slices
Tartar sauce
Seafood sauce

- ◆ Preheat the oven to 350°.
- ◆ Place the clams on a cookie sheet. Bake in oven until shells just open. Remove the clams from the shells and reserve the liqueur.
- ◆ Beat the eggs and liqueur in a bowl.
- ◆ In another bowl combine the bread crumbs and cayenne.
- ◆ Dip the clams first in the egg mixture, then bread crumbs.
- ◆ In a wok or large skillet heat 2 inches of oil to 375°.
- ◆ Fry the clams in the hot oil until just browned. Drain on paper towels.
- ◆ Serve with lemon slices, tartar sauce or seafood sauce.

SAUTEED OYSTERS

Serves 4

2 eggs	½ cup bread crumbs
¼ cup milk	½ cup panko
¼ cup parsley	1 quart oysters
1 teaspoon salt	Butter

- ◆ Beat the eggs and milk in a bowl until fluffy.
- ◆ In another bowl combine the parsley, salt, crumbs and panko.
- ◆ Dip the oysters in egg mixture. Roll oysters in parsley and bread crumbs. Saute in butter.
- ◆ Oysters can also be fried in oil.
- ◆ Serve with tartar sauce or horseradish sauce.

SALMON WITH BEURRE BLANC

Serves 4

1½ pounds salmon fillet	2 Tbls. olive oil
Juice of 1 lemon	

- ◆ Sprinkle the salmon with the lemon juice and olive oil. Grill on a BBQ until just browned.

Caper-Scallion Beurre Blanc

½ cup dry white wine	2 Tbls. capers
½ cup white wine vinegar	½ stick unsalted butter
2 Tbls. shallots, chopped	Salt, pepper to taste
1 scallion, chopped	

- ◆ In a small saucepan simmer the wine, vinegar, shallots and scallion. Reduce to ½. Beat in the butter. Season with salt, pepper and capers. Serve with the salmon.

SALMON WITH LOBSTER SAUCE

Serves 4

1 ½ pounds salmon fillet
¼ cup dry white wine

Juice of ½ lemon

- Preheat oven to 350°
- Place the salmon in a baking dish.
- Pour the wine and lemon juice over the salmon.
- Bake in oven for 15 minutes.
- Remove from dish and serve on individual plates with lobster sauce.

Lobster Sauce

¾ stick butter
1 scallion, chopped
2 large Portobello mushrooms, finely chopped
2 Tbls. flour
1 cup half and half

¼ cup champagne
½ pound lobster meat

- Melt the butter in a saucepan.
- Add the scallions and mushrooms.
- Stir in flour and then half and half.
- Add champagne and lobster

GRILLED SALMON

Serves

1½ pounds salmon filet
¼ cup lime juice

2 Tbls. olive oil
Crab imperial – p. 67

- Sprinkle the lime juice and olive oil on salmon.
- Grill salmon on BBQ.
- Remove from BBQ and place on platter.
- Serve with crab imperial.

SALMON AND SHRIMP BAKE

Serves 8

2 pounds salmon fillet
1 pound large shrimp

½ pound mushrooms
Chive cream sauce

- ♦ Preheat oven to 350°
- ♦ Place the salmon in a buttered baking dish. Top with shrimp, mushrooms and chive cream sauce.
- ♦ Bake ½ hour or until bubbling and just browned.
- ♦ Rockfish can be substituted for salmon, and crab for shrimp.

Chive Cream Sauce

1 stick butter
½ cup flour
2 cups half and half

4 chives, snipped
½ cup dry white wine

- ♦ Melt butter in a sauce pan. Stir in flour and half and half until thickened. Add chives and wine.

SALMON WITH BOURBON GLAZE

Serves 4

1½ pounds salmon fillet
Juice of 1 lemon

- ♦ Sprinkle the juice over the salmon.
- ♦ Grill or broil the salmon.
- ♦ Slice into 4 pieces. Serve with Bourbon Glaze.

Bourbon Glaze Sauce

2 cloves garlic, minced
2 Tbls. olive oil
2 Tbls. soy sauce
½ cup water

½ cup brown sugar
1 Tbls. lemon juice
¼ cup bourbon
½ cup toasted almond slices

- ♦ Combine all ingredients in a saucepan. Bring to a boil. Simmer for ½ hour.
- ♦ Serve over salmon slices topped with almonds.

PAELLA

Serves 6

¼ cup olive oil
2 boneless chicken breasts
½ pound chorizo
4 cloves garlic, minced
4 green onions, chopped
3 medium tomatoes, peeled and chopped finely
1 red pepper, chopped
2 stalks celery, chopped
3 cups water
1½ cups rice

2 teaspoons paprika
1 cube chicken bouillon
1 teaspoon tumeric
1 teaspoon chili powder
½ teaspoon saffron
1 pound shrimp, peeled and deveined
2 pounds mussels
½ cup peas
Salt and pepper to taste

- ◆ In a large sauce pan heat the olive oil. Add the chicken and chorizo until just browned. Remove from heat and put in a separate dish.
- ◆ Add the garlic, scallions, tomatoes, red pepper and celery to the pan. Add more olive oil if necessary. Saute until tender. Add the water, rice, paprika, bouillon, tumeric, chili powder and saffron.
- ◆ Add the chicken and chorizo. Bring to a boil. Reduce heat and simmer for 15 minutes.
- ◆ Add the shrimp, mussels and peas. Simmer for five minutes.
- ◆ Season with salt and pepper.
- ◆ Serve with crusty bread and a salad.

CODFISH BALLS

Serves 4

1 pound dried codfish
2 cups mashed potatoes
1 egg
2 green onions, chopped
2 cloves garlic, minced
¼ cup parsley, chopped

4 slices bacon, cooked and crumbled
½ cup cream
1 cup panko
2 Tbls. butter
2 Tbls. olive oil

- Place the codfish in a sauce pan. Cover with water. Bring to boil. Drain. Crumble cod into pieces.
- Combine the cod, mashed potatoes, egg, onions, garlic, parsley, bacon and cream in a bowl. Make into balls.
- Put the panko in a bowl. Dip the codfish balls in the panko.
- Heat the butter and olive oil in a skillet. Saute the balls until browned.
- Serve with salsa, tartar sauce or horseradish sauce.

BAKED CODFISH

Serves 6

6 red bliss potatoes
2½ pounds codfish filets
1 pound asparagus, cut in 2" pieces
3 cloves garlic, minced
1 cup leeks, chopped

2 Tbls. dill
1 teaspoon kosher salt
1 teaspoon pepper
½ cup white wine

- Preheat oven to 350°
- Blanch the potatoes in boiling water for five minutes.
- Place the fish in a greased baking dish. Top with other ingredients.
- Bake 20 minutes, or until bubbling.
- Serve with rice.

POULTRY

The author's paternal grandparents, Mr. and Mrs. William Hadwen
Barney of Hopedale and Nantucket

"Christmas won't be Christmas without any presents".
Little Women
Louisa May Alcott
(1832-1888)

From World War II to about 1975 the chicken industry in Maine was centered around Ellsworth. Today Belfast is still a major poultry center, and a port for exporting potatoes.

In 1888 the Weber brothers bought an incubator, 2 Peking drakes and ducks for $175 in Wrentham, MA. 600 ducklings were sold in 1890 for $1.20 each.

In 1985 Boston Chicken was founded in Newton, MA. The company was bought in 1991 and moved to Naperville, IL.

CHICKEN IN WATERCRESS SAUCE

Serves 6

½ stick butter
2 Tbls. olive oil
6 boneless chicken breasts
3 scallions, chopped
1 cup dry white wine

1 cup chicken stock
1 pound watercress (two large bunches), stems removed
1 cup heavy cream
Salt and pepper

- ◆ Heat the butter and oil in a Dutch oven or covered skillet Stir in the scallions. Add the chicken breasts and brown on each side. Stir in the wine and bring to a boil. Add the stock. Cover and cook for 30 minutes. Remove the chicken from the skillet.
- ◆ Add the watercress and cream. Simmer until slightly thickened.
- ◆ Return the chicken to the skillet.
- ◆ Serve with noodles or rice.

STUFFED CHICKEN

Serves 6

6 boneless chicken breasts
½ cup pecans
½ cup baby spinach

½ cup cranberries
¼ cup brown sugar
½ stick butter

- ◆ Preheat oven to 350°
- ◆ Pound chicken breasts to ¼ inch thickness.
- ◆ Combine pecans, spinach, cranberries, and sugar in a bowl.
- ◆ Divide up mixture on each chicken breast. Secure with toothpick. Place in baking dish. Dot with butter.
- ◆ Bake for 35-40 minutes or until just browned.
- ◆ Gruyere cheese can be substituted for the cranberries and brown sugar.
- ◆ Serve with cranberry chutney and rice.

CHICKEN WITH PEPPER SAUCE

Serves 6

½ cup olive oil
1 red pepper, sliced
1 green pepper, sliced
1 yellow pepper, sliced
4 scallions, sliced
4 cloves garlic, minced

6 boneless chicken breasts
1 cup dry white wine
3 large tomatoes, chopped
½ cup fresh basil
1 teaspoon salt
1 teaspoon ground pepper

- ◆ Heat ¼ cup oil in the skillet and add the peppers, scallions and garlic until soft. Remove and place in a bowl.
- ◆ Add the rest of the oil to the skillet and add the chicken. Brown on both sides.
- ◆ Add the peppers, onion and garlic to the pan. Pour in the wine and cook until reduced by half.
- ◆ Stir in the tomatoes, basil, salt and pepper. Cover and cook for 25 minutes.
- ◆ Serve with rice.

CHICKEN WITH APRICOT SAUCE

Serves 6

¼ cup flour
2 teaspoons curry powder
1 teaspoon pepper
1 teaspoon kosher salt
6 boneless chicken breasts
2 Tbls. olive oil
2 Tbls. butter

1 cup dried apricots
1 cup chicken broth
2 Tbls. tomato paste
½ cup dried cranberries
2 Tbls. sugar
2 scallions, chopped
½ cup toasted almonds

- ♦ Preheat oven to 325°
- ♦ In a bowl combine the flour, curry, pepper and salt. Dredge the chicken in the mixture.
- ♦ Heat the oil and butter in a skillet. Brown the chicken on each side, about 5 minutes per side. Remove chicken and place in a baking dish.
- ♦ Add the other ingredients, except almonds to skillet.
- ♦ Pour over the chicken.
- ♦ Bake for 1 hour. Remove from oven and top with almonds.
- ♦ Serve with rice, couscous or noodles.

LILI'S BARBECUED CHICKEN

Serves 6

6 boneless chicken breasts
¼ cup peanut butter
½ cup maple syrup
¾ cup ketchup
¼ cup Dijon mustard

1 small onion, chopped
1 Tbls. Worcestershire sauce
1 teaspoon salt
1 teaspoon pepper

- ♦ In a bowl combine all the ingredients. Refrigerate for at least two hours.
- ♦ Grill on BBQ for about 15 minutes per side, and browned.

GRILLED CHICKEN

Serves 4

4 boneless chicken breasts
½ cup olive oil
2 green onions, grated
2 cloves garlic, crushed
2 Tbls. mint, chopped

2 Tbls. cilantro, chopped
1 teaspoon paprika
¼ teaspoon cayenne
Salt and pepper

- ◆ In a bowl combine all of the ingredients. Let marinate at least 4 hours.
- ◆ Grill on BBQ for about 15 minutes per side or until golden brown.
- ◆ Serve with couscous and a Greek salad.

ROAST CHICKEN WITH LEMON SHERRY SAUCE

Serves 6

6 boneless chicken breasts
15 ounce can artichoke hearts
1 pound chorizo
2 roasted peppers, sliced
¼ cup fresh rosemary
1 stick butter

½ cup flour
2 cups chicken stock
1 cup heavy cream
Juice of 1 lemon
Zest of 1 lemon
¼ cup sherry

- ◆ Preheat oven to 350°.
- ◆ In a sauce pan melt the butter and stir in the flour. Add the chicken stock and cream. Stir until thickened. Add the lemon, lemon zest and sherry.
- ◆ Place the chicken breasts, artichoke hearts, chorizo, peppers and rosemary in a large Dutch oven or baking dish.
- ◆ Pour the sauce over the chicken.
- ◆ Bake for one hour.
- ◆ Serve with rice.

GRILLED CHICKEN PRIMAVERA

Serves 6

6 chicken breasts
¼ cup olive oil
1 zucchini, sliced
2 red bell peppers, sliced
1 large red onion, sliced

1 pound asparagus, sliced into
1" pieces
1 pound green beans
½ cup pesto (p. 31)
½ cup heavy cream
¼ cup dry white wine

- Sprinkle the chicken breasts with a small amount of salt and pepper. Grill the chicken breasts on a BBQ for about 15 minutes to a side and browned. Place on a serving platter.
- Heat ½ the oil in a skillet and add the zucchini, red pepper, onion, asparagus and green beans. Saute for 3 minutes. Remove from skillet and arrange around chicken on the serving platter.
- Using the rest of the oil in the skillet, stir in the pesto, heavy cream and white wine. Pour this sauce over the chicken and vegetables. Serve warm.
- This same recipe can be used as a one dish meal by adding 1 pound cooked pasta such as capellini.

GRILLED CHICKEN

Serves 4

¼ cup olive oil
1 Tbls. kosher salt
¼ cup lemon juice
1 Tbls. pepper
2 cloves garlic, minced
4 boneless chicken breasts
2 large red onion, sliced

1 pound portabella mushrooms, sliced
2 large tomatoes, sliced
2 red bell peppers, sliced
1 bunch basil, chopped
½ pound mozzarella, sliced

- Combine all ingredients, except basil and cheese in a bowl.
- Grill on a BBQ the chicken breasts for 15 minutes to a side.
- Grill vegetables.
- Place chicken topped with vegetables on a platter. Top each piece with basil and a slice of mozzarella.
- Serve with rice or couscous.

GRILLED CHICKEN BREASTS WITH GORGONZOLA

Serves 6

6 boneless chicken breasts
Salt and pepper
½ stick butter
1 pound fresh baby spinach

1 pound broccoli florets
½ pound Gorgonzola cheese
½ cup pine nuts

- ♦ Sprinkle the chicken breasts with a small amount of salt and pepper. Grill the chicken breasts on a barbecue until desired pinkness. Place on a serving platter.
- ♦ Melt the butter in a skillet. Add the spinach and broccoli and sauté for about 5 minutes, until just tender. Add the cheese and pine nuts until the cheese is just slightly melted.
- ♦ Spoon mixture on top of chicken breasts. Serve warm.

GRILLED CHICKEN BREASTS

Serves 6

¼ cup olive oil
¼ cup lemon juice
6 boneless chicken breasts
2 leeks, sliced lengthwise
1 pound baby spinach

2 Tbls. rosemary
1 cup toasted pinenuts
1 cup raisins
3 cups cooked rice

- ♦ Rub the chicken breasts with 2 Tbls. olive oil and 2Tbls. lemon juice.
- ♦ Grill on BBQ for about 15 minutes per side, or until browned.
- ♦ Heat the remained oil in a skillet. Stir in leeks and spinach until tender. Add rosemary, pine nuts, raisins and remaining lemon juice.
- ♦ Serve chicken breasts on bed of rice topped with leek mixture.

GRILLED CHICKEN

Serves 6

6 boneless chicken breasts
¼ cup olive oil
2 Tbls. tarragon vinegar
¼ cup lime juice

½ cup cilantro
1 pound cooked lima beans
3 cups cooked corn
3 tomatoes, chopped

- ◆ In a bowl combine the ingredients. Refrigerate for at least 2 hours.
- ◆ Grill the chicken on a BBQ, reserving marinade and vegetables.
- ◆ Serve chicken on a platter, top with vegetables and marinade.

CHICKEN WITH MUSTARD CREAM

Serves 6

6 boneless chicken breasts
3 cups cooked wild rice
1 pound mushrooms, sliced

2 bunches watercress, remove stems

- ◆ Preheat oven to 350°
- ◆ Place the rice in a greased casserole. Top with chicken breasts, mushrooms and sauce.
- ◆ Bake 45 minutes.
- ◆ Divide the watercress among six plates. Serve the chicken and wild rice on the watercress.
- ◆ Chicken and mushrooms also can be baked separately from wild rice. Serve over watercress with rice on side.

Mustard Cream Sauce

1 stick butter
½ cup flour
2 cups cream

¼ cup Dijon mustard
3 cloves garlic, minced
¼ cup white wine

- ◆ Melt the butter in a sauce pan. Stir in flour and cream until thickened. Add mustard, garlic and wine.

BAKED CHICKEN

Serves 6

6 boneless chicken breasts
2 eggs, beaten
½ cup flour

1 teaspoon nutmeg
½ cup Japanese bread crumbs
½ stick butter, melted

- Preheat oven to 350°.
- Place the eggs, flour and nutmeg, and Japanese bread crumbs each in separate bowls for dredging chicken breasts.
- First dredge the breasts in the beaten eggs, then flour and finally in the bread crumbs.
- Place in a baking dish and cover with butter. Bake for 1 hour.
- Serve with cranberry chutney.

CHICKEN WITH CILANTRO PESTO

Serves 4

4 boneless chicken breasts
¼ cup lime juice
2 Tbls. olive oil

1 cup sour cream
2 cups cooked rice

- In a bowl marinate the chicken, lime juice and olive oil for 2 hours refrigerated.
- Grill chicken on BBQ until browned on both sides.
- Place chicken on platter. Top with sour cream and pesto.
- Serve with rice

Cilantro Pesto

2 bunches cilantro, remove stems and chop
2 Tbls. olive oil
¼ cup lime juice

2 jalapeno, seeded and chopped finely
¼ cup pine nuts

- Combine all ingredients in a bowl.

CHICKEN CASSEROLE

Serves 4

½ stick butter
¼ cup flour
1½ cups cream
1 Tbls. curry
2 Tbls fresh grated ginger
¼ teaspoon cumin

2 cups cooked chicken, diced
½ cup coconut
¾ pound baby spinach
½ cup sliced almonds
2 cups cooked rice

- Preheat oven to 350°
- Melt the butter in a sauce pan. Stir in flour and cream until thickened. Add spices, chicken and coconut.
- Place the spinach in a greased casserole. Top with chicken mixture and garnish with almonds.
- Bake ½ hour, or until bubbling.
- Serve with rice.
- For a one dish meal, layer rice, spinach and chicken.
- Whole chicken breasts can be substituted for diced chicken.
- Apples and wild rice can be substituted for spinach and rice.

CHICKEN CASSEROLE

Serves 6

½ pound thin sliced Black Forest ham
6 boneless chicken breasts

1 pound wild mushrooms, sliced
Double recipe bearnaise sauce – p. 206

- Preheat oven to 350°
- Place the ham in a greased baking dish. Top with chicken breasts, mushrooms and béarnaise sauce.
- Bake 45 minutes or until just browned and bubbling.
- Serve with wild rice.

CHICKEN CASSEROLE

Serves 4

½ stick butter
4 shallots, chopped
¼ cup flour
1 cup cream
¼ cup dry white wine

Salt and pepper
1 pound asparagus
4 boneless chicken breasts
¼ cup basil, chopped
½ cup parmesan cheese

- Preheat oven to 350°
- Melt the butter in a sauce pan. Add shallots, flour and cream until thickened. Stir in wine, salt and pepper to taste.
- Put the asparagus in a greased baking dish and top with chicken. Sprinkle with basil. Pour cream sauce over basil. Finish with parmesan cheese.
- Bake 45 minutes, until just browned and bubbling.
- Serve with rice.
- Dill or tarragon can be substituted for basil.
- Sherry can be substituted for wine.

PEACHY CHICKEN

Serves 4

2 Tbls. butter
4 boneless chicken breasts
½ teaspoon allspice
2 Tbls. fresh grated ginger

4 peaches, peeled, pitted and sliced
1 cup peach preserves
1 cup pecans

- Preheat oven to 350°
- Put the butter in a baking dish and place in oven until butter is melted. Remove from oven.
- Place chicken in dish. Sprinkle each breast with allspice and ginger. Top with peaches, peach preserves and pecans.
- Bake 40 minutes, or until bubbling.

ROAST CHICKEN

Serves 6

1 large chicken

- ◆ Preheat oven to 500°
- ◆ Put chicken in baking dish. Stuff chicken cavity with stuffing I, II or III. Rub with small amount of butter and sprinkle with kosher salt.
- ◆ Bake 20 minutes. Reduce heat to 350°. Bake 1 hour.

Stuffing I

½ pound ground pork
1 cup ham, chopped
½ pound chorizo, chopped

½ cup raisins
2 hardboiled eggs, chopped
½ cup cheddar cheese

- ◆ In bowl combine all ingredients. Stuff chicken

Stuffing II

½ stick butter
1 small onion, chopped
2 shallot cloves, minced
½ pound mushrooms

2 cups fresh bread cubes
¼ cup Madeira
Salt and pepper

- ◆ Melt the butter in a skillet. Stir in onion, shallots, mushrooms and bread until bread is just lightly browned. Add Madeira, salt and pepper to taste.

Stuffing III

½ stick butter
2 cups cooked wild rice
1 cup bread, cubed
¼ cup orange juice

Zest of 1 orange
1 cup cranberries
2 Tbls. fresh grated ginger
½ teaspoon cinnamon

- ◆ Melt butter in a skillet. Stir in other ingredients until bread is just slightly browned.

STUFFED CORNISH HENS

Serves 6

3 Cornish hens
Stuffing III – p. 98

- ♦ Preheat oven to 350°
- ♦ Stuff hens with stuffing. Place on baking sheet. Sprinkle a small amount of kosher salt on each hen and a pat of butter.
- ♦ Bake 1 hour.
- ♦ Remove and place on platter. Reserve drippings.
- ♦ Serve with red wine sauce.

Red Wine Sauce

Drippings from hens
½ stick butter
1 Tbls. cornstarch

1 cup merlot
Salt and pepper to taste

- ♦ Warm the pan with the drippings on the stove. Add cornstarch and stir in wine until just slightly thickened. Add salt and pepper to taste.

GRILLED CORNISH HENS

Serves 6

3 large Cornish hens, cut in half
¼ cup olive oil

- ♦ Rub hens with olive oil.
- ♦ Grill on BBQ at least 20 minutes per side
- ♦ Serve with apple, walnut Calvados sauce – p. 205

GLAZED CORNISH HENS

Serves 6

3 large Cornish hens, cut in half   1 lemon, sliced
1 orange, sliced and seeded   Fresh mint

- ◆ Preheat oven to 350°
- ◆ In a shallow baking pan place the Cornish hens with skin side up. Brush with the glaze.
- ◆ Bake for 40 minutes.
- ◆ Garnish with the orange and lemon slices and fresh mint.

Glaze

½ cup Madeira   ½ cup orange juice
1 cup orange marmalade   1 teaspoon Dijon mustard

- ◆ In a bowl combine the Madeira, marmalade, orange juice and mustard.

PEPPER CRUSTED DUCK

Serves 4

1 5-6 pound duckling   ¼ cup fresh ground pepper
½ stick butter, softened   Fruit chutney – p. 204
1 Tbls. kosher salt

- ◆ Preheat oven to 500°
- ◆ Rub the duck with the softened butter and pepper. Sprinkle salt on duck. Place in baking dish.
- ◆ Roast for 20-25 or until browned. Reduce heat to 350°. Bake for 25 more minutes.
- ◆ Place on platter. Serve with fruit sauce.

ROAST TURKEY

20 pound turkey   Kosher salt

- ♦ Preheat oven to 500º.
- ♦ Place turkey in a covered roasting pan. Sprinkle with salt. Bake 20 minutes. Reduce heat to 350º and cook turkey 20 minutes to the pound.
- ♦ Place the giblets and neck in a pan of water. Bring to boil. Simmer until meat from neck falls off.
- ♦ Place turkey on large platter. Make gravy from drippings and giblet.

Wild Rice Stuffing

1 cup wild rice   ½ cup pecans
3 cups water   1 Tbls. poultry seasoning
1 teaspoon kosher salt   1 teaspoon thyme
1 stick butter   1 teaspoon dried dill
1 loaf French bread, cubed   ¼ cup fresh parsley
1 large onion, chopped   1 teaspoon fresh ground pepper
1 large stalk celery, diced

- ♦ In a sauce pan bring the water to a boil and add the rice. Reduce to simmer and cook 45 minutes.
- ♦ In a large skillet melt the butter and add the onion and celery, then the bread and just slightly brown. Add pecans, seasonings and wild rice.
- ♦ Stuff in both turkey crevices.

Portuguese Bread Stuffing

½ stick butter   1 cup cranberries
2 loaves Portuguese bread,   1 cup pecans
cubed   2 Tbls. fresh grated ginger
1 medium onion, chopped   1 Tbls. poultry seasoning
2 apples, peeled, cored and
chopped

- ♦ Melt the butter in a skillet. Add bread and onions, cooking until bread is just browned. Add other ingredients.
- ♦ Stuff turkey.

Apple Stuffing

1 pound chorizo, crumbled
½ stick butter
1 large loaf herb bread
1 small onion, chopped

2 apples, peeled, cored and
chopped
1 cup raisins
½ teaspoon sage
½ teaspoon thyme

- ♦ Heat the sausage in a skillet until just browned. Add butter, bread and onion, cooking until bread is just browned. Add other ingredients.
- ♦ Stuff turkey cavities.

Cornbread Stuffing

1 pound chorizo
½ stick butter
1 recipe cornbread, cut into
cubes
1 medium onion, chopped

2 stalks celery, chopped
1 cup cranberries
1 cup pecans
2 Tbls. fresh grated ginger

- ♦ Brown the chorizo in a skillet. Melt the butter in the skillet and add cornbread and onion. Cook until bread is just slightly browned. Stir in other ingredients.
- ♦ Stuff turkey cavities.

Oyster Stuffing

½ stick butter
1 loaf bread, cubed
1 large onion, chopped
1 large carrot, chopped
¼ cup parsley, chopped
1 pint oysters

1 teaspoon salt
1 teaspoon pepper
1 teaspoon thyme
½ teaspoon sage
1 cup chestnuts

- ♦ Melt butter in a skillet. Add bread and onion until bread until just browned. Add other ingredients.
- ♦ Stuff turkey cavities.

Cranberry Stuffing

1 pound chorizo
½ stick butter
1 medium red onion, chopped
1 load bread, cubed
1 cup pecans

1 cup cranberries
2 Tbls. fresh grated ginger
Zest of 1 orange
¼ cup orange juice

- ◆ Brown the sausage in a skillet. Melt butter in skillet. Add onion and bread. Cook until bread is just browned. Stir in other ingredients.
- ◆ Stuff turkey cavities.

Nut and Fruit Stuffing

½ stick butter
1 loaf bread
1 cup Brazil nuts
½ cup dried apricots

½ cup dried dates
½ cup dried cranberries
½ cup crystallized ginger

- ◆ Melt butter in a skillet. Stir in bread until just browned. Add other ingredients.
- ◆ Stuff turkey cavities.

GLAZED TURKEY

20 pound turkey

- ◆ Preheat oven to 350°
- ◆ Place turkey in a covered roasting pan. Cook 20 minutes per pound.

Maple Glaze

1 cup maple syrup
½ teaspoon vanilla
¼ teaspoon nutmeg

¼ teaspoon allspice
¼ teaspoon ginger
½ stick butter

- ◆ In a sauce pan combine all the ingredients. Glaze turkey with ½ mixture 1 hour before finished cooking, and rest of glaze ½ hour later.

ROAST GOOSE

Serves 6

1 6-8 pound goose	Grand Marnier Sauce or plum
Kosher salt	wine sauce

- Preheat oven to 325°
- Put goose in baking dish. Rub goose with salt. Stuff goose.
- Bake for 3 hours.
- Remove from oven and place on platter
- Pheasant or duck can be substituted for the goose.
- Serve with Grand Marnier or plum wine sauce.

Grand Marnier Sauce

½ stick butter	2 Tbls. brown sugar
¼ cup flour	Juice and rind of one orange
Goose drippings	Juice and rind of one lemon
1 cup beef stock	1 cup Grand Marnier
2 Tbls. tomato paste	2 Tbls. orange marmalade

- Melt butter in a sauce pan. Stir in flour, goose drippings, stock and tomato paste, until it thickens.
- Stir in other ingredients.
- Serve warm or chilled.

Cherry Wine Sauce

1 15 oz. can bing cherries	¼ cup orange juice
½ cup Port	Zest of 1 orange
¼ teaspoon cinnamon	½ cup red currant jam
¼ teaspoon ground cloves	

- Drain the cherries, reserving ½ the syrup.
- In a sauce pan warm the syrup, Port, cinnamon, cloves and orange juice until reduced in half. Remove from heat and add zest and jam.

MEATS

The author is also descended from the Brown family. She is pictured here in front of Brown University at the time of the 350th anniversary of the founding of Rhode Island.

The first three heifers and a bull were exported from England to Massachusetts in 1624 on board the English vessel, *Charity*. Vermont not only has numerous dairy farms, but sheep and cattle have been raised in the state for many years. Merino sheep were brought to Weathersfield Bow, VT in 1811 by William Jarvis who had been the U.S. consul to Portugal. The first cows were brought to Maine in 1634 and onloaded on the banks of the Salmon Falls River in South Berwick. Springfield, MA, founded in 1636 would later become a meat packing center.

Along the coast are found marsh grass "sea meadows" that provided hay for cattle. The grass had to be harvested in the mud, but was free feed.

The Billings Farm and Museum in Woodstock, VT was created by the Rockefeller family in 1982. Frederick Billings came to live in Woodstock in 1861, and in 1871 established the farm, raising Jersey cattle from the Isle of Jersey. Today the working farm is open to the public.

In 1867 William Underwood & Company introduced canned deviled ham.

In 1963 Julia Child first appeared on TV in Boston demonstrating Boeuf Bourguignon.

HERB CRUSTED BEEF

Serves 6

2½ pounds beef tenderloin
1 Tbls. dried mustard
¼ cup butter, melted
½ cup fresh bread crumbs
½ cup watercress, finely chopped
½ cup fresh parsley, finely chopped
2 cloves garlic, minced
2 Tbls. fresh ground pepper
1 container boursin cheese

- ♦ Preheat the oven to 400°
- ♦ In a bowl combine the mustard, butter, bread crumbs, watercress, parsley, garlic and pepper to form a paste. Rub the tenderloin with the mixture.
- ♦ Roast the tenderloin for 30-40 minutes or desired pinkness.
- ♦ Place on a platter. Serve the boursin in a side bowl.

BEEF WITH PORT SAUCE

Serves 6

2½ pounds beef tenderloin

- ◆ Grill the tenderloin on a BBQ until desired pinkness. Serve with sauce.
- ◆ Lamb or pork can be substituted for the beef

Apple/Blackberry Port Sauce

1 cup redcurrant jelly
1 cup port
1 Tbls. shallot, chopped
¼ cup orange juice

Juice of 1 lemon
½ apple, diced
1 pint blackberries

- ◆ Melt the jelly in a sauce pan. Add the other ingredients. Bring to a boil.

BEEF WITH CARAMELIZED ONIONS

Serves 6

2 ½ pounds beef tenderloin
3 large onions, sliced thinly
½ stick butter
¼ cup sugar

½ pound blue cheese
6 slices bacon, cooked and crumbled

- ◆ Grill the tenderloin on a barbecue until desired pinkness. Remove and place on a platter. Slice.
- ◆ In a skillet melt the butter and add the onions, stirring until very limp. Add the sugar.
- ◆ Crumble the blue cheese and bacon on top of the tenderloin slices. Top with the caramelized onions. Serve immediately.

BEEF TENDERLOIN WITH GORGONZOLA SAUCE

Serves 6

2 ½ pounds beef tenderloin
¼ cup fresh ground pepper

2 Tbls. garlic salt
2 Tbls. kosher salt

- ◆ In a bowl combine the pepper, salt and garlic salt.
- ◆ Rub the beef with the pepper mixture.
- ◆ Grill the beef until desired pinkness.
- ◆ Serve with Gorgonzola Sauce.

Gorgonzola Sauce

1 stick butter
½ cup flour
1 cup heavy cream
1 cup half and half

2 Tbls. shallots, chopped
½ pound Gorgonzola
¼ cup Port

- ◆ In a sauce pan melt the butter. Stir in the flour and the cream and half and half. Add the shallots and Gorgonzola, and stir until the sauce is smooth. Stir in port.

BEEF TENDERLOIN WITH MUSHROOM DEMI GLACE

Serves 6

2½ pounds beef tenderloin
1 Tbls. kosher salt
2 Tbls. pepper

2 Tbls. Dijon mustard
1 pound wild mushrooms sliced
½ cup Port or red wine

- ◆ Preheat broiler.
- ◆ Rub the tenderloin with salt, pepper and mustard. Set meat in roasting pan.
- ◆ Broil until desired pinkness. Place meat on platter. Reserve juices in roasting pan.
- ◆ Put the pan on the stove top and heat juices. Stir in mushrooms for 2 minutes. Add Port. Pour sauce over meat.

BEEF TENDERLOIN

Serves 6

2½ pounds beef tenderloin   2 Tbls. kosher salt
2 Tbls. freshly ground pepper

- ♦ Coat the beef with the salt and pepper. Cook on the grill until desired pinkness. Remove and place on a platter.
- ♦ Serve with herb sauce or smoked bacon sauce.
- ♦ Pork tenderloin or boneless leg of lamb can be substituted for the beef.

Herb Sauce

¼ cup shallots, chopped   1 teaspoon thyme
2 Tbls. butter   2 teaspoons fresh rosemary
2 Tbls. fresh ground pepper   1 teaspoon marjoram
1 cup beef broth   ¼ cup bourbon

- ♦ Melt the butter in a sauce pan and add the shallots, sauteing until just tender. Add the other ingredients, except bourbon. Bring to a boil. Remove from heat and add bourbon.
- ♦ Serve in a gravy boat with the beef.
- ♦ The sauce can be thickened with just a slight amount of flour.

Smoked Maple Bacon Bourbon Sauce

¼ cup maple syrup   6 slices smoked maple bacon,
½ cup bourbon   cooked and crumbled
½ stick butter

- ♦ In a sauce pan heat the maple syrup, bourbon and butter to boiling.
- ♦ Place in a gravy boat and sprinkle with bacon.

BEEF STEW

Serves 6

6 slices bacon
1 large onion, peeled and sliced
2 ½ pounds stewing beef, cut into cubes
¼ cup flour
1 cup Burgandy
½ stick butter
2 large carrots, peeled and sliced
2 jalapeno chilis, seeded and chopped

½ pound portabella mushrooms, sliced
2 large tomatoes, chopped
3 cloves garlic, chopped
2 leeks, sliced
2 celery stalks, chopped
¼ cup fresh parsley
2 bay leaves
½ teaspoon thyme
1 teaspoon salt
2 teaspoons fresh ground pepper

- Fry the in a Dutch oven. Remove and reserve fat. Cut bacon into small pieces. Place in bowl.
- Saute the onions in the fat until translucent. Remove to bowl with bacon.
- In a bowl coat the beef cubes in the flour.
- Melt the butter in the skillet and add beef, cooking until just browned. Add wine and stir in all the other ingredients. Bring to a boil. Cover and simmer until meat and vegetables are tender, about 1 ½ hours.

CHILI

Serves 8

3 pound ground beef
2 large onions, chopped
6 large cloves garlic, minced
3 jalapenos, seeded and chopped
2 Tbls. chili powder
1 Tbls. ground cumin
1 Tbls. oregano

1 Tbls. coriander
1 cup dark beer
6 large tomatoes, finely chopped
2 cans kidney beans
8 slices bacon, cooked and crumbled
Salt and pepper

- In a large pot brown the meat and onions. Add the other ingredients. Bring to a boil. Reduce to simmer, stirring all the ingredients together for 50 minutes.

RED FLANNEL HASH

Serves 4

2 cups corned beef, cooked and diced
2 cups potatoes, cooked and diced
1 cup beets, cooked and diced

1 medium onion, chopped
Salt and pepper to taste
3 tablespoons butter
¼ cup cream

- ◆ In a bowl combine the corned beef, potatoes, onions, and beets. Sprinkle with the salt and pepper.
- ◆ Melt the butter in an iron skillet. Add the meat and vegetable mixture.
- ◆ Pour in the cream. Flatten mixture with a spatula.
- ◆ Cook until browned. Turn and brown on other side.
- ◆ Serve on individual plates with poached eggs on top and ketchup.

STEAK AND MUSHROOM PIE

Serves 4

2 Tbls. olive oil
4 strips bacon
1½ pounds sirloin, cut into small cubes
¼ cup flour
½ cups beef stock
½ pound baby onions, frozen or canned

½ pound cremini mushrooms, sliced
¼ cup fresh basil
¼ cup red wine
Pie crust
1 egg, beaten

- ◆ Preheat the oven to 350°
- ◆ In a skillet brown the bacon. Remove. Add the olive oil to the skillet
- ◆ In a bowl toss the flour and steak cubes. Brown the steak in the skillet. Stir in the beef stock until thickened.
- ◆ Add the onions, mushrooms, and fresh basil. Stir in the wine.
- ◆ Place in a casserole and top with the pie crust. Brush the crust with the beaten egg.
- ◆ Bake in the oven for 40 minutes or until crust is slightly browned.
- ◆ Serve with a salad and red wine for a hearty meal.

CRANBERRY SPICED MEATBALLS

Makes 12 meatballs

2 pounds ground beef
4 green onions, chopped
1 cup cranberries
2 Tbls. fresh grated ginger

1 teaspoon cumin
½ cup slivered almonds
1 egg, beaten

- ◆ Combine the ingredients in a bowl. Shape into balls.
- ◆ Fry in a skillet until desired pinkness.
- ◆ Ground lamb can be substituted for the beef.

MEATLOAF

Serves 4

1 ½ pounds ground sirloin
1 egg
1 small onion, chopped
1 ½ cups fresh bread crumbs

1 teaspoon kosher salt
1 teaspoon fresh ground pepper
½ cup ketchup or tomato sauce

- ◆ Preheat oven to 350º.
- ◆ In a bowl combine all the ingredients.
- ◆ Place in baking dish and pack tightly.
- ◆ Bake 1½ hours.

Tomato Sauce

½ cup ketchup or tomato sauce
2 Tbls. white wine vinegar
¼ cup dark brown sugar

½ cup water
2 teaspoons Dijon mustard
1 Tbls. Worcestershire sauce

- ◆ In a sauce pan spoon combine all the ingredients. Spoon ½ tomato sauce over meatloaf before baking. Add rest of ingredients after 1 hour.

LEG OF LAMB WITH MINT SAUCE

Serves 8

1 cup dry white wine
¼ cup fresh mint chopped
4 cloves garlic, grated
1 Tbls. coarse salt

1 Tbls. fresh ground pepper
Juice of 1 lemon
4 pound boneless leg of lamb

- In a large baking dish combine all the ingredients and add the lamb. Marinate overnight.
- Cook on grill until desired pinkness basting with the marinade.

Mint Sauce

1 cup sour cream
¼ cup fresh mint

Juice of 1 lemon
4 cloves garlic, minced

- Combine all the ingredients in a bowl and serve with the lamb.

LAMB WITH CURRANT SAUCE

Serves 8

3 ½ pounds boneless leg of lamb
4 large cloves garlic, grated

¼ cup fresh ground pepper
2 Tbls. Kosher salt

- Rub the lamb with the garlic, pepper and salt. Cook on a grill to desired pinkness. Place on a platter and serve with currant sauce.

Currant Sauce

8 oz. currant jelly
3 Tbls. Brandy

¼ cup fresh mint

- In a sauce pan melt the currant jelly. Add the brandy and mint. Serve in a bowl with the lamb.
- Cranberry chutney can be substituted for the currant jelly.

LAMB KEBAB

Serves 8

3 pounds lamb cubes
2 Tbls. kosher salt
2 Tbls. fresh ground pepper
¼ cup lemon juice
4 cloves garlic, minced
¼ cup fresh oregano, chopped

1 large onion, peeled and cut
into small cubes
2 large tomatoes
1 red pepper, cut into cubes
1 green pepper, cut into cubes
1 zucchini, cut into cubes
8 artichoke hearts

- ◆ In a bowl combine the salt, pepper, lemon juice, garlic and oregano. Add the lamb and coat on all sides. Refrigerate at least one hour.
- ◆ On large skewers alternate lamb and vegetables.
- ◆ Grill until vegetables are tender and meat is cooked to desired pinkness. Baste with left over marinade.
- ◆ Serve with couscous and mint sauce.

GROUND LAMB PATTIES

Serves 6

2 ½ pounds ground lamb
1 Tbls. Kosher salt
1 Tbls. fresh ground pepper

3 cloves garlic, minced
6 hardboiled eggs

- ◆ In a bowl combine the lamb, salt, pepper and garlic. Shape lamb into patties and place on a platter.
- ◆ Make a hole in each patty and add one whole egg, shaping lamb to close in egg.
- ◆ Grill each patty until desired pinkness.
- ◆ Serve with Dijon mustard or sour cream seasoned with mint or coriander, chopped scallion, and 1 chopped jalapeno chili.
- ◆ Blue cheese, chopped onions, raisins, or black olives can be substituted for the eggs.

LAMB WITH SPINACH

Serves 6

2 ½ pounds boneless lamb
tenderloin, cubed
2 Tbls. fresh grated ginger
1 Tbl.s fresh thyme
1 teaspoon kosher salt
2 Tbl.s fresh ground pepper
¼ cup olive oil

1 medium onion, chopped
4 cloves garlic, crushed
1 large tomato, peeled and finely
chopped
2 ½ cups water
1 pound fresh spinach

- In a covered bowl combine the ginger, thyme, salt and pepper. Add the lamb cubes and refrigerate overnight.
- Heat the oil in the skillet and add the onion and garlic. Stir for 5 minutes.
- Add the lamb and tomatoes until the meat is just slightly browned.
- Add the water. Cover and simmer for 30 minutes. Stir in the spinach until thickened.
- Serve with coucous, rice or noodles.

LAMB STEW

Serves 6

2 ½ pounds lamb, cut into cubes
3 large tomatoes
1 small eggplant, peeled and cut
into cubes
1 small zucchini, peeled and cut
into cubes
2 large potatoes, peeled and cut
into cubes

1 large onion, peeled and cut
into cubes
2 cloves garlic, grated
1 teaspoon cinnamon
½ teaspoon nutmeg
½ teaspoon cloves
½ cup white wine

- In a Dutch oven combine all the ingredients. Heat on stovetop to boiling. Cover and simmer until the lamb is tender, about 1½ hours. Stir to keep from sticking.
- This can also be baked in a 350° for 1 ½ hours or until meat is tender.
- Garnish with fresh parsley and serve with French bread or on top of noodles.

GRILLED LAMB

Serves 8

3 pounds boneless leg of lamb   2 Tbls. kosher salt
¼ cup pepper   2 Tbls. garlic powder

- ◆ Rub the meat with the pepper, salt and garlic.
- ◆ Grill on BBQ for 45 minutes, turning frequently, or until desired pinkness. Serve with Rockefeller Sauce or red pepper sauce.

Rockefeller Sauce

½ stick butter   1 15 oz jar marinated artichoke
1 pound baby spinach   hearts, drained
4 green onions, chopped   ¼ cup parsley, chopped
                                       1 cup parmesan cheese

- ◆ Melt the butter in a sauce pan. Stir in spinach, onions, artichoke hearts and parsley, until spinach is just wilted. Stir in cheese.
- ◆ Place in bowl.

Red Pepper Mint Sauce

2 red bell peppers, roasted and   ¼ cup mint, chopped
finely chopped   ¼ teaspoon cayenne
¼ cup olive oil   2 green onions, chopped

- ◆ Combine ingredients in a bowl.

Peach Sauce

3 ripe peaches, peeled, pitted   ¼ cup mint
and sliced   2 Tbls. fresh grated ginger
¼ cup lime or lemon juice

- ◆ Grill peach slices in grill basket just before cooking leg of lamb. Remove from basket and chop finely. Put in a bowl. Add other ingredients.

RACK OF LAMB

Serves 4

2 ½ lbs. rack of lamb (8 ribs)	1 Tbls. kosher salt
2 Tbls. rosemary	2 Tbls. oregano
2 Tbls. pepper	1 Tbls. garlic salt

- ♦ Preheat oven to 350°
- ♦ Combine the herbs, garlic, salt and pepper in a bowl. Rub the lamb with the mixture.
- ♦ Place in baking dish and bake 1 hour. Place on platter and save drippings.

Cabernet Sauce

½ stick butter	Lamb drippings
2 Tbls. shallots, chopped	1 cup cabernet
2 Tbls. flour	1 Tbls oregano

- ♦ Melt the butter in a sauce pan. Stir in shallots and flour. Add drippings, cabernet and oregano. Stir until just slightly thickened.

BAKED PORK CHOPS

Serves 8

8 loin pork chops	1 cup brown sugar
¼ cup olive oil	1 cup raisins
Salt and pepper	½ cup dark rum
4 apples, cored and sliced	

- ♦ Preheat oven to 350°
- ♦ In a skillet heat the olive oil.
- ♦ Sprinkle salt and pepper on the pork chops. Brown the pork chops in the skillet. Transfer to a large baking dish. Top with the apples.
- ♦ In a bowl combine the brown sugar, raisins and rum. Pour over the pork chops. Bake 20 minutes or until bubbling.

PORK WITH APPLES

Serves 8

½ stick butter
2 ½ pounds pork tenderloin, cut into cubes
2 pounds baby onions (canned or frozen)
2 cups apple cider
1 cup beef stock

3 apples, cored, peeled and sliced
1 cup cranberries
2 Tbls. fresh grated ginger
Zest of 1 lemon
1 cup whipping cream

- Heat the butter in a large skillet and brown the pork cubes. Remove pork to a bowl.
- Brown the onions in the skillet and add lemon, cider and beef stock. Bring to a boil.
- Return the pork to the pan with the apples and cranberries. Simmer for ½ hour. Add the cream.
- Serve warm with noodles.

PORK TENDERLOIN WITH FRUIT

Serves 8

3½ pounds boneless pork tenderloin
½ cup brown sugar
1 cup red currant jam.
½ cup red wine

1 cup dried apples
1 cup dried apricots
1 cup dried prunes
1 cup dried currants

- Preheat oven to 350°.
- In a roasting pan cook the tenderloin for 1½ hours or until desired pinkness. Remove from pan and place on a warm platter.
- Place the pan on the top of the stove. Heat currant jam and red wine until the jam is melted. Add the other ingredients and stir until fruit is just tender.
- Place sauce in a bowl and serve with the tenderloin

PORK TENDERLOIN

Serves 8

3½ pounds pork tenderloin
¼ cup freshly ground black pepper

2 Tbls. dry mustard
½ teaspoon cayenne
2 Tbls. Kosher salt

- In a bowl combine the pepper, mustard, cayenne and salt. Rub the meat with this mixture.
- Cook the pork on a grill until the desired pinkness.
- 2 Tbls. thyme, 2 Tbls. basil, 2 Tbls. garlic salt, 2 Tbls. black pepper can be substituted for the above dry rub.

Cranberry Sauce

2 cups cranberries
¼ cup Port
1 cup water

½ cup sugar
Zest of 1 orange
Juice of 2 large oranges

- In a sauce pan combine the cranberries, water and sugar. Bring to a boil and berries begin to pop.
- Remove from heat and add zest, orange juice and Port.
- Pour into gravy boat and serve warm with the pork.

Plum Sauce

½ stick butter
4 scallions, chopped
8 oz. plum preserve
4 whole plums, peeled, pitted and chopped

¼ cup fresh lemon juice
½ cup brown sugar
2 Tbls. soy sauce
1 Tbls. dry mustard
Pinch of cayenne

- Melt the butter in a sauce pan and saute scallions until just tender. Stir in the ingredients over low heat until plums are tender and the sauce is thickened.
- Serve in a bowl with the tenderloin.

Mustard Sauce

1 cup whipping cream
¼ cup coarse mustard

Salt and pepper to taste
¼ Champagne or dry white wine

- ◆ In a bowl beat the cream until peaks form. Stir in the other ingredients so mixture is just blended.
- ◆ Serve in a bowl with the tenderloin.

BAKED HAM

1 8 pound ham shank

- ◆ Preheat oven to 350°
- ◆ Place the ham in a roasting pan. Pour ½ glaze over ham.
- ◆ Bake 1 hour. Pour rest of glaze over the ham. Bake ½ more.
- ◆ Serve ham with mustard and apple butter.

Maple Glaze

½ cup maple syrup
½ cup orange juice
Zest of 1 orange

¼ teaspoon cloves
½ teaspoon cinnamon

- ◆ Combine the ingredients in a sauce pan. Heat to boiling.

VEAL WITH DILL SAUCE

Serves 6

2 ½ pounds veal scallopini
¼ cup flour

½ stick butter
Salt and pepper

- In a bowl combine the flour, salt and pepper. Dredge the veal in the mixture.
- In a skillet heat the butter. Add a few pieces of veal and just brown on each side.
- Remove veal and place on a warm platter. Reserve drippings in skillet.
- Serve the veal with fettuccine or other pasta.

Dill Sauce

¼ cup sour cream
½ cup heavy cream

¼ cup fresh dill
Juice of 1 lemon

- Stir the ingredients into the veal drippings in the skillet. Heat until just warmed.
- Serve over the veal, or in a separate bowl.

SPINACH AND CHORIZO

Serves 6

½ stick butter
1½ pounds fresh spinach
4 cloves garlic, crushed

2 pounds chorizo
¼ cup dry white wine
Salt and pepper

- In a skillet melt the butter. Stir in the garlic and add the spinach until just wilted. Add the chorizo, wine, and salt and pepper to taste.

VEGETABLES

When we visited Nantucket as children everyone dressed to the nines on the airplane ride. Here we are greeted by Azzie, my grandmother's wonderful cook and Uncle Randy Sharp.

Myles Standish explored Cape Cod before settling in Plymouth. In Truro they stumbled on Native American graves and a cache of corn which they plundered. The spot is marked with a plaque at Corn Hill.

The potato was introduced in Boston in 1718 by an Irish Presbyterian minister. The potatoes were used for cattle fodder for over a century. The 1840's brought a large number of Irish immigrants, especially to Boston during the Great famine in Ireland. In 1719 potatoes were planted in Londonderry, NH. Potatoes are grown in the northernmost part of Maine, mainly in Aroostook County, and shipped from Caribou. Fort Fairfield has an annual potato festival with a Little Miss Potato Blossom contest and Maine Potato Queen Pageant.

The Winooski River in Vermont comes from the Native American name for "onion". Wethersfield, CT developed the Wethersfield Red Onion, a precursor to the Bermuda onion.

Broom corn was introduced to Hadley, MA in 1791, and later broom straw. Hadley then became the asparagus capital and grew onions also. The soil was rich with nutrients from the annual flooding of the Connecticut River. Today the Hadley Farm Museum displays early agricultural products and implements.

In 1796 Joel Barlow, a Connecticut poet wrote "The Hasty Pudding". Hasty pudding is cornmeal mush cooked until thickened. Indian Pudding is similar but made with spices and sweetened.

Isaac Winslow of Maine received a patent for an "Improved Process of Preserving Green Corn" in 1862. Twelve cans of the corn were sold to S.S. Pierce of Boston.

In 1863 Fearing Burr, Jr. of Hingham, MA published The Field and Garden Vegetables of America.

In 1867 George Burnham and Charles S. Morrill of Portland, ME established a cannery on Casco Bay. In 1870 the company became Burnham & Morrill and became famous for its oven baked beans. The world's first canned baked beans were produced by B&M in 1875 for the Maine fishing fleet. In 1926 Burnham & Morrill began selling B&M Brick Oven Baked Beans. The plant was moved to East Deering, ME in 1955 by which time it was producing baked beans, pork and beans, and brown breads.

In 1872 Luther Burbank, a Massachusetts horticulturist, developed the Idaho potato.

In 1930 Birds Eye Frosted Foods were introduced in Springfield, MA by General Foods. The first precooked frozen foods marketed under the Birds Eye label are chicken fricassee and crisscross steak.

In 1941 the House of McCormick built a potato dehydration plant in Maine. The company was one of the early developers of DDT.

In 1971 Shepard and Linette Erhart founded the Maine Coast Sea Vegetables company in Franklin, ME to market seaweed for the Japanese.

BAKED BEANS

2 pounds navy beans
8 slices bacon, cut in pieces
1 medium onion, chopped
1 green pepper, chopped
¾ cup dark molasses
½ cup brown sugar

1 Tbls dried mustard
¼ teaspoon cloves
1 teaspoon salt
1 teaspoon pepper
½ cup red wine

- Wash beans in cold water and soak overnight. Drain.
- Place the beans in a Dutch oven. Cover with water. Bring to a boil. Cook about 35 minutes or until beans are tender.
- Add rest of ingredients. Stir to make sure beans are thoroughly coated.
- Preheat oven to 300°.
- Bake beans in middle of oven for 5 hours. Add more water or wine if mixture starts to become dry.
- Serve the beans from the pot.

TOMATO PIE

Serves 4

Pastry

1¼ cups flour
1 stick butter

¼ cup cold water
3 Tbls. cream cheese

- ♦ Preheat the oven to 400°
- ♦ Blend all the ingredients in a food processor. Roll into pie crust shape and place in pie plate.
- ♦ Bake for 10 minutes. Remove from oven.

Filling

3 large tomatoes, sliced
¼ cup basil, chopped
3 chives, snipped

3 scallions, chopped
1 cup mayonnaise
1 cup cheddar cheese, grated

- ♦ Place the tomatoes in the pie crust. Top with other ingredients, finishing with cheese.
- ♦ Bake 20 minutes or until just browned and bubbling.

STUFFED TOMATOES

Serves 6

6 tomatoes, cored. Save tomato pulp
½ pound baby spinach
3 Tbls. tarragon, snipped
3 Tbls. dill, snipped

¼ cup parsley, chopped
3 cloves garlic, minced
Salt/pepper to taste
1 cup parmesan cheese

- ♦ Preheat oven to 350°
- ♦ In a bowl combine all ingredients, except tomatoes and cheese.
- ♦ Stuff tomatoes with mixture and top with cheese.
- ♦ Bake 20 minutes, or until just bubbling.

LOBSTER MASHED POTATOES

Serves 6

6 large baking potatoes
½ cup half and half
½ stick butter
½ teaspoon salt
½ teaspoon pepper

2 scallions, chopped
½ pound lobster meat
Basil leaves
Sour Cream

- ◆ Preheat oven to 350°
- ◆ Bake the potatoes for 1 hour. Remove from oven. Remove top part of skin and scoop out pulp. Reserve skins.
- ◆ In a bowl combine the pulp, half and half, salt, pepper and scallions. Gently fold in the lobster. Spoon back into the skin.
- ◆ Bake 15 minutes, or until just bubbling and slightly browned.
- ◆ Garnish with the basil leaves and sour cream.

POTATO PUFFS

Serves 6

This is a good way to use up leftover mashed potatoes, or make them fresh.

3 cups mashed potatoes
½ pound grated cheddar cheese
1 scallion, chopped

2 cloves garlic, crushed
2 eggs

- ◆ Preheat the oven to 425°.
- ◆ Grease a 12 muffin tin.
- ◆ In a bowl combine all the ingredients. Spoon the mixture into the tins.
- ◆ Bake for 15 minutes or until browned.

POTATO LEEK DISH

Serves 4

½ stick butter
¼ cup flour
1½ cups half and half
½ teaspoon nutmeg

1 cup Gruyere
4 large russet potatoes, peeled and sliced
1 cup leeks, chopped

- Preheat oven to 350
- Melt the butter in a sauce pan. Stir in flour and half and half until thickened. Add nutmeg and Gruyere.
- Place the potatoes in a greased baking dish. Top with leeks and sauce.
- Bake ½ hour or until bubbling and slightly browned. Serve hot.

BAKED POTATOES

Serves 6

6 medium baking potatoes
1 cup milk
½ stick butter
1 teaspoon salt
1 teaspoon pepper
¼ cup parsley, chopped

1 green pepper, chopped
2 green chilis, seeded and finely chopped
1 large tomato, chopped
1 cup Monterey Jack cheese

- Preheat oven to 400
- Place the potatoes in a microwave on high for 10 minutes. Prick to make sure they are tender. Remove.
- Cut top off potato and remove pulp. Save skins. Place pulp in a bowl. Mash with milk, butter, salt and pepper.
- Put mashed potatoes back in skins. Divide rest of ingredients among the potatoes.
- Bake 15 minutes, or until just browned and bubbling.

BAKED POTATOES WITH SAUSAGE

This is a meal served with a salad and Italian bread.

Serves 6

6 medium baking potatoes
1 cup milk
½ stick butter
1 teaspoon salt
1 teaspoon pepper
3 cloves garlic, minced
3 green onions, chopped

1 Tbls. Italian herbs
1 pound chorizo sausage, browned and cut in pieces
1 cup tomato sauce
1 cup mozzarella cheese, shredded

- ♦ Preheat oven to 400
- ♦ Place the potatoes in a microwave on high for 10 minutes. Prick to make sure they are tender. Remove.
- ♦ Cut top off potato and remove pulp. Save skins. Place pulp in a bowl. Mash with milk, butter, salt, pepper and garlic.
- ♦ Put mashed potatoes back in skins. Divide rest of ingredients among the potatoes.
- ♦ Bake 15 minutes, or until just browned and bubbling.

SWEET POTATO CHIPS

Serves 4-6

2 pounds sweet potatoes
Vegetable oil

- ♦ Wash the sweet potatoes and cook in boiling water for 10 minutes. Drain. Slice very thin. Dry with paper towel.
- ♦ Heat the oil in a fryer to 375°. Deep fry the potatoes a small amount at a time for about 2 minutes. Drain on a paper towel. Put back in for another 2 minutes. Crisp and just browned.
- ♦ Serve immediately.

SWEET POTATO CASSEROLE

Serves 6

4 large sweet potatoes
2 apples, peeled, cored and sliced
1 cup orange juice
½ cup maple syrup
½ teaspoon ginger
1 teaspoon cinnamon
½ teaspoon nutmeg
2 Tbls. fresh grated ginger
¼ teaspoon cloves
1 cup raisins
½ stick butter
Zest of 1 orange
1 cup pecans

- ♦ Preheat oven to 350°
- ♦ Boil the sweet potatoes until tender. Remove skins.
- ♦ Place potatoes in greased baking dish. Mash. Add other ingredients.
- ♦ Bake ½ hour, or until bubbling.

FRIED EGGPLANT

Serves 6

1 large eggplant, cut in half lengthwise, with each half cut in 12 pieces
1 Tbls. kosher salt
1 cup flour
1 teaspoon cumin
¼ teaspoon red pepper
½ cup cold water
2 eggs
Vegetable oil

- ♦ Place the eggplant in a large bowl and sprinkle with salt.
- ♦ In another bowl combine the flour, cumin, red pepper, eggs and water.
- ♦ Pour the vegetable oil into a large skillet. Heat the oil, but do not let splatter.
- ♦ Dip the eggplant into the batter. Fry the eggplant in the hot oil, until browned on both sides.
- ♦ Transfer to a dish lined with paper towels.
- ♦ Serve warm with tomato sauce or salsa.

STUFFED EGGPLANT

Serves 8

4 medium size eggplant
¼ cup olive oil
1 large onion, peeled and chopped
1 red pepper, seeded and chopped
1 green pepper, seeded and chopped

4 cloves garlic, minced
8 plum tomatoes, chopped
½ cup fresh basil chopped
Salt and pepper
½ cup fine bread crumbs
½ cup fresh grated parmesan cheese
Lemon juice

- ♦ Preheat the oven to 375°.
- ♦ Cut the eggplant in half and remove flesh. Reserve shells.
- ♦ Heat the olive oil in a skillet and stir in onions and peppers. Add garlic, tomatoes, eggplant flesh and basil. Add salt and pepper to taste.
- ♦ In a bowl combine the bread crumbs and cheese.
- ♦ Stuff the eggplant shells with the tomato mixture. Pour the cheese-bread crumb mixture on top.
- ♦ Drizzle olive oil and lemon juice over the eggplant.
- ♦ Place eggplant on baking sheet. Cover and cook for 50 minutes
- ♦ Garnish with fresh basil or parsley.

BEANS IN TOMATO SAUCE

Serves 6-8

1 pound dried giant white beans
3 medium onions, chopped
3 large carrots, peeled and sliced
3 large tomatoes, peeled and chopped

Salt and pepper
¼ cup parsley, finely chopped
1 cup olive oil

- ♦ The night before serving the dish, soak the beans in a large bowl of water. Boil them the next morning for an hour, or until tender. Drain water and reserve beans.
- ♦ In a large sauce pan simmer the onions, carrots, tomatoes, salt, pepper, parsley and olive oil for 30 minutes. Add the beans.
- ♦ Serve warm.

CURRIED VEGETABLES

Serves 6-8

½ stick butter
1 medium onion, peeled and chopped
2 Tbls. fresh ginger
2 cloves garlic, minced
1 teaspoon salt
1 teaspoon cumin
½ teaspoon tumeric

Pinch of red pepper
Pinch of cayenne
1 Tbls. curry powder
4 medium tomatoes, chopped
2 cups green peas
3 large potatoes, cut into cubes
1 cup water
¼ cup fresh cilantro, chopped

- ♦ In a large pan heat the butter and saute the onions until they are just browned. Add the garlic and ginger.
- ♦ Stir in the cumin, tumeric, red pepper, cayenne and curry powder. Add the tomatoes and stir until thickened about 5 minutes. Add the potatoes and peas, and coat them with the tomato mixture. Add the water and bring to a boil. Cover and reduce heat. Simmer until the potatoes and peas are tender. Add the cilantro. Serve hot.

SKEWERED VEGETABLES

Serves 6-8

1 large eggplant, cut into cubes
1 zucchini, cut into cubes
1 yellow squash, cut into cubes
1 large red onion, peeled and cubed
1 red pepper, cut into cubes
1 green pepper, cut into cubes
1 pound cremini mushrooms, tops only

Juice of 1 lemon
¼ cup olive oil
¼ cup soy sauce
4 cloves garlic, minced
2 Tbls. fresh tarragon, chopped
2 Tbls. fresh basil, chopped
2 Tbls, fresh thyme, chopped
1 teaspoon salt
1 Tbls. fresh ground pepper

- ♦ In a large bowl combine the lemon juice, olive oil, soy sauce, garlic, herbs, salt and pepper. Let marinate in the refrigerator for several hours.
- ♦ Thread the vegetables on skewers.
- ♦ Grill for about 15 minutes on each side, basting with the remaining marinade.

BRAISED RED CABBAGE

Serves 6

2 pounds red cabbage, shredded
2 medium onions, chopped
2 large apples, peeled, cored, and chopped
½ teaspoon nutmeg
½ teaspoon ground cloves

½ teaspoon cinnamon
2 Tbls. brown sugar
¼ cup red wine vinegar
2 Tbls. butter
Salt and pepper

- Preheat the oven to 325°
- In a large covered casserole layer the cabbage with the onions, apples and spices. Pour the vinegar on top and the butter.
- Bake for 1 hour or until the cabbage is tender.

CABBAGE AND APPLES

Serves 4

½ stick butter
1 pound red cabbage, shredded
¼ cup lemon juice

2 large apples, peeled, cored and diced
¼ cup red currant jelly
4 cloves

- In a large sauce pan melt the butter and add the other ingredients. Bring to a boil.
- Simmer for 15 minutes, or until the cabbage is tender.

STUFFED MUSHROOMS

Serves 8

8 large portabella mushroom
caps
½ pound hot Italian sausage or
chorizo

½ pound sun-dried tomatoes
½ pound provolone cheese,
grated

- ♦ Preheat the oven to 350°.
- ♦ In a skillet brown the sausage. Add the sun-dried tomatoes
- ♦ ntil just tender. Remove from heat.
- ♦ Stuff the mushroom caps with the sausage mixture. Sprinkle with the cheese.
- ♦ Place the mushrooms on a baking pan. Bake for 15 minutes or until just tender.
- ♦ Spoon the sauce over the mushrooms. Serve warm.

Tomato Sauce

4 large plum tomatoes, finely
chopped

½ cup white wine
2 Tbls. fresh sage

- ♦ Combine the ingredients in a bowl.

SAUTEED CORN

Serves 4-6

½ stick butter
1 small onion, chopped
3 cups fresh corn
¼ cup green pepper, finely
chopped

¼ cup red pepper, finely
chopped
2 tomatoes, chopped
¼ cup fresh basil, chopped
Salt and pepper to taste

- ♦ In a skillet melt the butter and sauté the onion. Add the other ingredients.
- ♦ Stir until just tender, about 5 minutes. Serve warm.

CHEESE POLENTA

Polenta is nothing more than a cornmeal mush. You can buy it in most markets, but it is a very easy and good dish to prepare. It is very much like grits, which has to be doctored up with butter and cheese to even taste good. However polenta can be made without the cheese and fried or baked. Serve this with maple syrup.

Serves 4-6

1 cup cornmeal
¾ cup water
3 ¼ cups water
½ teaspoon salt

2 Tbls. butter
1 cup sharp cheddar cheese, grated

- ◆ Preheat oven to 350°
- ◆ In a sauce pan bring the water to a boil. Add the cornmeal. Cook until the mixture thickens. Cover and remove from heat.
- ◆ Add the other ingredients. Pour into a greased 9" baking dish. Bake for 15-20 minutes or until bubbly.
- ◆ You can also add chopped jalapenos, chopped red or green pepper for more flavor.
- ◆ Swiss, Jarlsberg or parmesan cheese can be substituted for the cheddar.

SPINACH CASSEROLE

Serves 6

2 pounds baby spinach
8 ounces cream cheese
6 slices bacon, cooked and crumbled

3 scallions, chopped
2 Tbls. horseradish
Salt/pepper

- ◆ Preheat oven to 350°
- ◆ In a casserole combine all the ingredients. Bake 25 minutes, or until bubbling.

SPINACH QUICHE

Serves 4

Pie crust – p. 125
3 eggs
½ cups half and half
1 pound baby spinach

½ pound porcini mushrooms,
sliced
¼ cup fresh basil, chopped

- ◆ Preheat oven to 400°
- ◆ In a bowl beat the eggs and half and half.
- ◆ Place the spinach, mushrooms and basil in pie crust. Pour the egg mixture over the top.
- ◆ Bake 45 minutes, or until set.
- ◆ 1 cup Gruyere or Swiss cheese can also be added.

SOUFFLED SQUASH

Serves 4

2 cups yellow squash, cooked,
drained and mashed
½ cup celery, chopped
½ cup onion, chopped
1½ cups milk
3 eggs

1 cup bread crumbs
1 cup cheddar cheese
1 Tbls. dill
1 Tbls. tarragon
1 Tbls. basil

- ◆ Preheat oven to 400°
- ◆ Combine ingredients in greased baking dish.
- ◆ Bake 30 minutes.

ACORN SQUASH WITH CRANBERRIES

Serves 6

3 large acorn squash, cut in half and seeded
1½ cups cranberries

¼ cup maple syrup
1 cup pecans
½ stick butter, melted

- ◆ Preheat oven to 350°.
- ◆ Place the squash on a baking tray. Bake for 20 minutes. Remove from oven.
- ◆ In a bowl combine the cranberries, maple syrup, pecans and butter. Divide evenly among the squash.
- ◆ Place squash back in oven and cook for 20 minutes or until the squash is tender.

STUFFED ACORN SQUASH

Serves 6

3 acorn squash
½ cup raisins
½ cup brown sugar
2 cups diced apples

¼ cup fresh lemon juice
½ cup cranberry chutney
½ stick butter, melted

- ◆ Preheat oven to 350°.
- ◆ Cut the acorn squash lengthwise in half. Remove the seeds. Place on a baking sheet.
- ◆ In a bowl combine the raisins, brown sugar, apples, lemon juice, chutney and butter. Stuff each of the squash with the raisin mixture.
- ◆ Bake for 20 minutes.

SAUTEED GREEN BEANS

Serves 6-8

½ stick butter
2 pounds fresh green beans
½ pound chorizo, diced

½ pound ham, diced
¼ cup dill, snipped

- ◆ Melt the butter in a skillet. Stir in beans. Saute 3 minutes. Add chorizo, ham and dill.
- ◆ Serve hot or chilled.

PARSNIPS IN ORANGE SAUCE

Serves 4

½ stick butter
2 Tbls. honey
1 teaspoon cinnamon
2 Tbls. orange zest
1 cup orange juice

1 pound fresh parsnips, peeled and sliced lengthwise
Orange slices
Fresh mint

- ◆ Melt the butter and honey in a skillet. Add the cinnamon and orange zest. Stir in the orange juice and parsnips. Bring to a boil and cover. Cook for 25 minutes or until the parsnips are tender.
- ◆ Place in a serving dish. Garnish with the orange slices and fresh mint.

CRANBERRY MAPLE CARROTS

Serves 6

½ stick butter
3 large carrots, peeled and sliced
1 cup cranberries

½ cup maple syrup
1 cup pecans

- ◆ Melt the butter in a skillet. Add carrots and cook 3 minutes. Stir in cranberries, maple syrup and pecans.

CORN FRITTERS

2 cups fresh corn
1 teaspoon salt
½ cup milk
2 eggs, beaten
¼ cup green pepper

¼ cup sweet red pepper
¼ cup cilantro, chopped
1 cup flour
1½ teaspoons baking powder

- ◆ In a bowl combine all the ingredients.
- ◆ Heat 2 Tbls. butter in a skillet.
- ◆ Drop the corn mixture by large spoonfuls into the skillet. Cook until just browned on each side.
- ◆ For a spicier taste add 1 jalapeno, seeded and chopped finely and ¼ cup fresh cilantro.
- ◆ These are good served with salsa or maple syrup.

FRIED CILANTRO

2 bunches cilantro
Oil

- ◆ Heat the oil in a skillet.
- ◆ Drop in the cilantro.
- ◆ Fry until just slightly browned.
- ◆ Serve with curry or other spicy dishes.

DILLED CUCUMBERS

Serves 4

2 cucumbers, sliced thinly
2 Tbls. chives, snipped
2 Tbls. dill, chopped

¾ cup yogurt
Salt and pepper

- ◆ Place the cucumbers in a bowl and salt. Refrigerate covered for at least two hours.
- ◆ Combine with the other ingredients and serve immediately.

SALADS

The author and her grandmother Barney at the Barnacle

In 1981 Paul Newman began producing Newman's Own Oil-and-Vinegar Salad Dressing in Westport, CT. After tax profits were donated to charity.

LOBSTER CAESAR SALAD

Serves 4

3 cloves garlic, crushed
1 Tbls. kosher salt
½ teaspoon pepper
Juice of 1 large lemon, about ¼ cup
¼ cup olive oil

1 head romaine lettuce
1 pound lobster meat
1 cup herb bread croutons
1 cup grated parmesan cheese
¼ cup basil, chopped

- ♦ Rub the garlic around the sides of a large salad bowl, and then salt and pepper. Stir in lemon juice and olive oil.
- ♦ Tear the lettuce into pieces and add to bowl. Spoon lobster on lettuce. Top with croutons and cheese. Garnish with basil.

GRILLED SCALLOP SALAD

Serves 4

1½ pounds sea or Bay scallops
¼ cup lemon juice
2 Tbls. olive oil

Pesto – p. 31
1 pound cheese tortellini
4 Boston lettuce leaves

- ♦ In a bowl combine the scallops, lemon juice and olive oil.
- ♦ Grill the scallops, or broil until just browned.
- ♦ Cook tortellini according to instructions. Drain.
- ♦ Place the lettuce leaves on 4 plates. Divide up scallops and pour pesto on scallops.

GRILLED SCALLOP SALAD

Serves 4

1½ pounds scallops
¼ cup lime juice
2 Tbls. olive oil
2 Tbls. balsamic vinegar
2 Tbls. lemon juice

2 bunches watercress
1 large red onion, sliced
1 pound asparagus, cut in 2"
pieces, blanched

- Marinate the scallops in lime juice in a bowl for at least 2 hours refrigerated
- Grill scallops on a BBQ until just browned.
- In a bowl combine the olive oil, vinegar and lemon juice.
- Arrange the watercress on 4 plates. Top with one slice onion, asparagus, and scallops. Drizzle dressing over salad.

SCALLOP SALAD

Serves 4

1½ pounds sea scallops
Maple smoked bacon
2 shallots, chopped
¼ cup parsley
2 Tbls. rice vinegar

2 Tbls. olive oil
¼ cup lemon juice
½ pound mixed spring greens
½ cup toasted almonds

- Preheat broiler
- Cut the bacon pieces in half and wrap around each scallop. Secure with a toothpick.
- Place under broiler until bacon is just crisp.
- In a bowl combine the shallots, parsley, vinegar, olive oil and lemon juice.
- Arrange the mixed greens on 4 plates. Top with scallops. Drizzle dressing over scallops. Sprinkle with almonds.
- Bay scallops can be substituted for sea scallops. Cut the bacon in thirds.

CARAMELIZED SEA SCALLOPS

Serves 8

5 cups onions, thinly sliced
3 tablespoons butter
1 tablespoon olive oil
1 teaspoon salt
¼ teaspoon sugar
½ cup dry white wine
½ cup honey
2 Tbls. olive oil

¼ cup lemon juice
3 ½ pounds sea scallops
1 large head bibb lettuce
2 cucumber, sliced
2 red bell peppers, sliced
¼ cup toasted sesame seeds

- ♦ Cook onions in butter and olive oil in covered pan for 15 minutes, stirring occasionally. Uncover, raise heat and stir.
- ♦ Add salt and sugar. Cook 30-40 minutes until onions are a deep golden brown. Add wine. Cook for 3 minutes.
- ♦ In a bowl combine the honey, olive oil, lemon juice and scallops.
- ♦ Broil or grill scallops until just browned.
- ♦ Place 1 leaf of bibb lettuce on each plate. Divide onions and scallops among each plate. Garnish with cucumber slices, sliced peppers and top with sesame seeds. Drizzle a small amount of honey mixture over each plate.

SEAFOOD SALAD

Serves 6

1 pound medium shrimp, cooked, peeled and deveined
1 pound crab meat
1 pound smoked salmon, cut into pieces
¼ cup lemon juice
¼ cup olive oil
¼ cup dill, snipped

½ pound feta, crumbled
6 romaine lettuce leaves
3 medium tomatoes, sliced
1 red onion, sliced
1 cucumber, sliced
1 pint bean sprouts
6 hardboiled eggs, cut in fourths
6 lemon slices

- ♦ In a bowl combine the shrimp, crab and salmon with the lemon juice, olive oil, dill and cheese.
- ♦ Arrange the lettuce leaves on six plates. Put some of the seafood on each plate. Garnish with other ingredients.

CRANBERRY SALAD MOLD

Serves 4

2 cups cranberries
2 oranges, peeled and sectioned

1 lemon, sliced thinly
½ cup sugar

- ◆ Combine the ingredients in a bowl and chill for two hours.

2 enveloped unflavored gelatin
½ cup cold water
1 cup hot water
½ cup pecans

1 apple, peeled, cored and
chopped finely
1 celery stalk, chopped

- ◆ Dissolve the gelatin in cold water. Add hot water.
- ◆ In a bowl combine all ingredients, including cranberry mixture.
- ◆ Pour into a mold. Chill for at least 4 hours.
- ◆ Unmold and serve on a bed of lettuce with a bowl of mint cream – 1 cup whipped cream, 12 mint leaves, and ¼ cup sugar folded in.

GREEN SALAD

Serves 4

1 medium head Boston lettuce
2 green onions, chopped
12 grape tomatoes
1 small cucumber, sliced
1 red bell pepper, sliced
2 Tbls. basil, chopped

2 Tbls. tarragon, chopped
2 Tbls. parsley, chopped
¼ cup olive oil
2 Tbls. tarragon vinegar
1 teaspoon sea salt
1 teaspoon fresh ground pepper

- ◆ Toss all ingredients in a salad bowl.

HEARTS OF PALM

Serves 4

1 can hearts of palm, sliced   ¼ cup lemon juice
16 cherry tomatoes   ¼ cup olive oil
1 medium red onion, chopped
½ pound mushrooms, sliced

♦ Toss all ingredients in a bowl.
♦ Courtesy of Angela Porta of Stamford

SUMMER SALAD

Serves 6

1 purple pepper, sliced   1 cup fresh peas
1 red pepper, sliced   ½ cup fresh basil, chopped
2 large tomatoes, sliced   Juice of 1 lemon
1 large cucumber, peeled and   2 Tbls. olive oil
sliced   1 teaspoon fresh ground pepper
2 scallions, sliced   ½ teaspoon kosher salt
1 cup fresh corn

♦ In a bowl combine the lemon juice, olive oil, salt pepper and basil.
♦ Add the vegetables and toss. Serve chilled.

GREEN BEAN SALAD

Serves 6

1½ pounds fresh green beans
2 red peppers, sliced
2 scallions, chopped
24 pitted black or Greek olives
¼ cup cilantro, chopped

¼ cup balsamic vinegar
¼ cup olive oil
¼ teaspoon kosher salt
½ teaspoon fresh ground pepper

- ◆ Blanche beans in boiling water for 3 minutes. Drain and cool.
- ◆ Toss the ingredients in a salad bowl.

BEAN SALAD

Serves 8 or more

2 cups chick peas, cooked or canned
2 cups black-eyed peas, cooked or canned
2 cups red kidney beans
3 large cloves garlic, minced
¼ cup olive oil

3 scallions, chopped
2 jalapeno chiles, seeded and chopped
1 teaspoon kosher salt
2 teaspoons fresh ground pepper
¼ cup fresh lemon juice
¼ cup fresh cilantro chopped

- ◆ Combine all the ingredients in a bowl and refrigerate at least one hour or overnight. Serve chilled.

FRUIT AND NUT SALAD

Serves 6

¼ cup mayonnaise
1Tbls.curry
¼ cup sour cream
1 head Boston lettuce
1 cup coconut, toasted

1 cup cashew nuts
3 large apples, peeled, cored and
sliced thinly
1 cup currants

- ♦ Combine the mayonnaise, curry, and sour cream in a bowl.
- ♦ In a salad bowl arrange the lettuce leaves.
- ♦ In a bowl combine the nuts, apples and currants with the mayonnaise mixture. Spoon onto the lettuce leaves.
- ♦ Top with the coconut.

BEET AND STILTON SALAD

Serves 4

24 baby beets, cooked and
peeled (can also be purchased
canned)
¼ cup Sherry vinegar
2 Tbls. olive oil

2 Tbls. lemon juice
¼ pound English Stilton
½ cup pecans
1 pound arugula

- ♦ In a bowl combine the beets, vinegar, olive oil and lemon juice. Marinate fro at least 2 hours.
- ♦ In a salad bowl toss all ingredients.

BEET SALAD

Serves 6

12 beets
½ cup olive oil
¼ cup balsamic vinegar
½ teaspoon kosher salt
½ teaspoon fresh ground pepper
½ pound marscapone
2 green apples, cored and thinly sliced

- Remove the tops from the beets.
- Cook the beets in boiling water in a sauce pan until just tender. Remove from the pan and cool. Remove the skins. Slice thinly and place in a bowl with the oil, vinegar, salt and pepper. Refrigerate for at least two hours.
- Arrange the beets on a serving platter, edge with apple slices.
- Make small round balls with the marscapone. Place on top of the beets.
- Serve immediately or the apples will become beet red.

COUNTRY SALAD

Serves 6

4 Vidalia onions, sliced
4 large beets, cooked, peeled and sliced
½ pound maple smoked bacon, cooked and crumbled
1 pound mixed spring greens
1 cup croutons
¼ cup olive or walnut oil
3 Tbls. balsamic vinegar
Zest of 1 orange

- Place the onions and beets in a grill basket. Grill on BBQ until onions are just browned and tender. Remove from grill.
- In a bowl toss together all ingredients.
- Onions and beets can also be roasted in the oven at 400°.
- Walnuts and blue cheese can also be added to salad.

COLE SLAW

Serves 4

1 cup blue cheese, crumbled	3 cups white cabbage, shredded
½ cup sour cream	3 cups red cabbage, shredded
2 Tbls. lemon juice	4 scallions, sliced
1 Tbls. sugar	Salt/pepper to taste

 ◆ Toss all ingredients in a bowl. Serve chilled.

ENDIVE AND SPINACH SALAD

Serves 6

1 Tbls. Dijon mustard	crumbled
¼ cup olive or walnut oil	1 cup candied pecans – p. 209
2 Tbls. raspberry vinegar	3 apples or pears, peeled, cored
2 Tbls. lemon juice	and sliced
2 pints raspberries	1 pound baby spinach
½ pound Gorgonzola cheese,	12 medium endive leaves

 ◆ Combine the mustard, oil, vinegar, lemon juice and 1 pint raspberries in a food processor.
 ◆ Toss together all ingredients in a salad bowl.

BROCCOLI SALAD

Serves 4

1 pound broccoli florets	cooked and crumbled
1 large red onion, sliced	½ cup mayonnaise
1 cup raisins	2 Tbls. sugar
1 cup pecans	¼ cup vinegar
4 slices maple smoked bacon,	

 ◆ Toss all ingredients in a salad bowl.

WILD RICE SALAD

Serves 4

2 cups cooked wild rice
1 cup walnuts
½ pound sun-dried tomatoes
¼ cup parsley

¼ cup olive oil
2 Tbls. red wine vinegar
Salt/pepper to taste

- Combine all ingredients in a salad bowl or serving dish.
- Cranberries can be substituted for the tomatoes.

CUCUMBER RING

Serves 4

2 packages unflavored gelatin
½ cup water
2 cups sour cream
2 Tbls. lime juice
2 Tbls. chives

2 cups cucumbers, diced
2 Tbls. tarragon vinegar
¾ cup sliced almonds
¼ cup sugar

- Soften gelatin in water. Stir in sour cream and lime juice. Add other ingredients. Pour into mold.
- Refrigerate for at least 4 hours.

CUCUMBER SALAD

Serves 6

2 large cucumbers, sliced
1 Tbls kosher salt
1 cup sour cream

2 Tbls. vinegar
1 large red onion, sliced

- Combine all ingredients in a bowl. Refrigerate for at least 2 hours.

SPINACH SALAD

Serves 6

6 slices bacon
1 pound baby spinach
1 pint bean sprouts
1 can sliced water chestnuts
6 hard boiled eggs, sliced
½ pound mushrooms, sliced

1 red onion, sliced
2 cups croutons
¼ cup vinegar
2 Tbls. lemon juice
1 Tbls. sugar

- ◆ Cook the bacon until crisp. Reserve fat. Crumble bacon.
- ◆ Toss all ingredients, including fat in a salad bowl.

BABY SPINACH SALAD

Serves 6

1 pound baby spinach
2 cups French bread croutons
6 slices bacon

6 hard boiled eggs
½ pound blue cheese, crumbled

- ◆ Toss all ingredients in a bowl all ingredients with dressing.

Sour Cream Dressing

½ cup sour cream
½ cup mayonnaise
¼ cup vinegar

1 Tbls. sugar
2 cloves garlic

- ◆ In a bowl combine the ingredients.
- ◆ Mozzarella or gorgonzola cheese can be substituted for the blue cheese.

SPINACH SALAD

Serves 4

1 pound baby spinach	1 cup spiced pecans – p. 209
4 oranges, peeled and sectioned	1 large red onion, sliced

- ◆ Toss the ingredients in a bowl with the cranberry vinaigrette.

Cranberry Vinaigrette

¼ cup honey	2 Tbls. balsamic vinegar
1 cup cranberries	2 Tbls. lemon juice

- ◆ Combine ingredients in food processor.
- ◆ Blueberries or other fruit can be substituted for the cranberries

SUMMER SALAD

Serves 8

1 pound romaine lettuce, torn	2 teaspoons fresh tarragon
1 head red leaf lettuce, torn	¼ cup fresh parsley
4 green onions, chopped	¼ cup olive oil
1 pound grape tomatoes	¼ cup tarragon vinegar
1 red pepper, sliced	1 teaspoon kosher salt
1 yellow pepper, sliced	1 teaspoon fresh ground pepper
¼ cup fresh basil, chopped	

- ◆ Toss together the ingredients in a salad bowl.

PORTABELLA SALAD

Serves 6

¼ cup olive oil
6 large portabella mushrooms,
without stems
3 cloves garlic

1 pound mixed spring greens
½ pound gorgonzola cheese,
crumbled

- ♦ Heat the oil and sauté the mushrooms and garlic.
- ♦ Place mushrooms on platter or plates with spring greens. Sprinkle the cheese in cavity.
- ♦ Mushrooms can also be placed under broiler with cheese until cheese melts.

FRUIT SALAD

Serves 8-10

1 head romaine lettuce, broken
1 cup dried cranberries
1 cup dried apricots
1 cup pitted dates

2 apples, cored and thinly sliced
1 medium red onion, peeled and
thinly sliced
1 cup walnuts

- ♦ Combine all the ingredients in a salad bowl. Toss with the dressing.

Poppy Seed Dressing

¼ cup olive oil
2 Tbls. cider vinegar

¼ cup honey
2 teaspoons poppy seeds

- ♦ Combine all the ingredients in a bowl. Pour over the salad.

PASTAS AND RICE

The Prince Macaroni Company was founded on Prince Street, Boston in 1912 and eventually moved to Lowell.

The North End of Boston was settled in 1631, but has always been a refuge for immigrants. By 1800 most residents were English or African. During the 1840s the Irish descended on the region, to be followed by the Italians. Today the North End is still known for its good and bountiful Italian food.

The author and her husband, George, at the Barnacle

LOBSTER ALFREDO

Serves 4

1 pound linguine
½ stick butter
2 green onions
2 cloves garlic, minced
1 cup cream

1 pound lobster meat
¼ cup parsley, chopped
1 teaspoon pepper
1 cup Asiago or parmesan cheese, grated

- ♦ Cook linguine according to directions. Drain.
- ♦ Melt butter in saucepan. Stir in onions and garlic. Add cream, lobster, linguine, parsley and pepper.
- ♦ Serve in individual pasta bowls with cheese.

LOBSTER FETTUCCINE

Serves 4

1 pound fettuccine
½ stick butter
2 Tbls. flour
1 cup cream
¼ cup dry white wine
1 pound thin spring asparagus,
cut in 2" pieces and blanched

2 large tomatoes, chopped
2 cloves garlic, minced
1 pound lobster meat
1 cup parmesan cheese, grated
Basil leaves

- ♦ Cook the fettuccine according to instructions.
- ♦ Melt the butter in a sauce pan. Stir in flour and cream until just slightly thickened. Add sherry, asparagus, tomatoes, garlic and lobster.
- ♦ Divide fettuccine between 4 bowls. Spoon lobster mixture on top.
- ♦ Garnish with cheese and basil leaves.

LOBSTER IN TARRAGON SAUCE

Serves 8

2 pounds bow tie pasta
½ stick butter
2 medium Vidalia onions, sliced
2 red peppers, sliced
2 pounds baby spinach

1 pound cremini mushrooms,
sliced
2 pounds lobster meat, shrimp or
scallops
8 lemon slices and basil leaves

- Cook the pasta according to directions. Drain.
- Melt the butter in skillet and add onions and peppers, stirring for 3 minutes. Stir in spinach and mushrooms, until spinach wilts.
- Place the spinach mixture on a platter or on 8 plates. Top with, pasta, lobster, tarragon sauce and basil leaves.

Tarragon Cream Sauce

1 stick butter
½ cup flour
2 cups cream

¼ cup Sherry
2 Tbls. tarragon
Salt/ pepper to taste

- Melt the butter in a sauce pan. Stir in flour and cream until thickened. Add Sherry, tarragon, salt and pepper. More tarragon can be added for a stronger flavor, but you do not want to overwhelm the lobster.

LOBSTER RISOTTO

Serves 4

2 Tbls. butter
1 small leek, chopped
2 cups arborio rice
3 cups chicken stock, warmed

½ pound thin spring asparagus,
cut in 1" pieces
1 pound lobster
½ cup basil, chopped
1 cup Asiago cheese, grated

- Melt the butter in a sauce pan. Stir in leek and rice. Slowly stir in stock, a small amount at a time, until rice is just crunchy. Add asparagus and lobster.
- Spoon risotto into pasta dishes and garnish with basil and cheese.

GARLIC MUSSELS

Serves 4

1 pound linguine
4 dozen mussels
¼ cup basil or parsley, chopped
¼ cup olive oil

2 large tomatoes, chopped
4 cloves garlic, minced
2 shallots, chopped
2 cups Chardonnay

- ♦ Combine all the ingredients, except linguine, in a large pot. Bring to a boil and mussels open. Discard any unopened mussels.
- ♦ Divide the fettuccine among 4 bowls. Top with mussels.
- ♦ Serve with crusty bread and salad.

MUSSELS AND FETTUCCINE

Serves 4

1 pound fettuccine
4 dozen mussels
¼ cup olive oil
4 cloves garlic, minced
Pinch of saffron
¼ cup basil

1 medium onion, chopped
2 large tomatoes, chopped
¼ cup lemon juice
2 cups white wine
Parmesan cheese

- ♦ Cook the fettuccine according to instructions. Drain
- ♦ In a large pot heat the olive oil. Stir in the onions and then add the garlic, saffron, basil and tomatoes. Gently fold in the mussels, white wine and lemon juice until mussels open.
- ♦ Divide the fettuccine among 4 pasta bowls. Pour mussels over pasta.
- ♦ Serve with fresh grated parmesan cheese.

MUSSELS AND ORZO

Serves 4

4 dozen mussels	4 cloves garlic, minced
2 cups white wine	¼ cup parsley, chopped
½ stick butter	2 Tbls. dill, snipped
1 onion, chopped	1 cup white wine
4 scallions, chopped	½ pound orzo

- Cook the orzo according to directions.
- Steam the mussels in the white wine, until shells open. Remove one shell from each mussel. Save wine.
- Melt the butter in a skillet. Saute the mussels with onions, scallions, garlic, parsley and dill for 3 minutes. Add wine and orzo.
- Stuff the mussel shells with the mixture.
- These can also be put under the broiler to just brown. Sprinkle some breadcrumbs on top.

SEAFOOD LINGUINE

Serves 8

1 pound salmon filets	4 green onions, chopped
1 pound cod filets	2 pounds linguine
1 pound bay scallops	1 pound parmesan cheese, grated
1 pound medium shrimp	
1 pound crab meat	Herb cream sauce – p. 207
1 pound mushrooms, sliced	
4 tomatoes, chopped	

- Grill all the seafood, except crab on a BBQ.
- Cook pasta in a sauce pan according to instructions. Drain and put in bowl.
- Using same pan melt butter and stir in mushrooms, tomatoes and onions. Cook for 3 minutes.
- Add fish, mushrooms and tomatoes to pasta. Pour herb sauce over top. Sprinkle parmesan cheese over sauce.
- Serve immediately.

GRILLED SEAFOOD OVER PASTA

Serves 6

2 dozen littleneck clams
1 pound shrimp, cooked, peeled
and deveined
1 pound bay or sea scallops
½ pound prosciutto, cut into
small strips

3 tomatoes, chopped
½ cup basil, chopped
1½ pounds spinach fettuccine
¼ cup olive oil
¼ cup lemon juice
1½ cups Asiago cheese, grated

- ♦ On the BBQ grill the clams, scallops and shrimp until just browned and clams open.
- ♦ Cook the fettuccine according to directions. Drain.
- ♦ In a large pasta bowl combine all the ingredients. Sprinkle the cheese on top.

SEAFOOD PASTA

This a hearty one dish meal, served with crusty bread.

Serves 6

¼ cup olive oil
1 small leek, chopped
1 pound mushrooms, sliced
½ pound baby spinach
1 15 oz. can artichoke hearts,
drained
3 large tomatoes, chopped

½ cup basil
3 cloves garlic minced
1 pound medium shrimp,
cooked, peeled and deveined
1 pound bay or sea scallops
1 pound lobster meat
1½ pounds linguine

- ♦ Cook linguine according to directions. Drain
- ♦ Heat the olive oil in a skillet. Saute leeks and mushrooms for 3 minutes. Add spinach, artichokes, tomatoes, basil and garlic. Stir in seafood.
- ♦ Put the linguine in individual pasta bowls. Pour seafood over linguine.
- ♦ Grated cheese or extra basil can be used to garnish pasta.
- ♦ Clams, mussels and other seafood can also be added.

SEAFOOD WITH LOBSTER SAUCE

Serves 6

1½ pounds capellini	¼ cup basil, chopped
1 stick butter	¼ cup Sherry
½ cup flour	1 pound medium shrimp,
2 cups cream	cooked, peeled and deveined
2 medium tomatoes, chopped	1 pound bay or sea scallops
3 cloves garlic, minced	1½ pounds lobster meat

- Cook the capellini according to instructions. Drain
- Grill the scallops and shrimp on the BBQ.
- Melt the butter in a sauce pan. Stir in flour and cream until thickened. Add tomatoes, garlic, basil, Sherry and ½ pound lobster meat.
- In a large pasta bowl or individual bowls divide the capellini. Divide seafood among bowls. Top with lobster sauce.
- Crab meat can be substituted for the lobster.
- Grated cheese can also be served with the pasta.

POLENTA SEA SCALLOPS

Serves 4-6

2 pounds sea scallops	Polenta – p.190 – double recipe

- Grill sea scallops on BBQ.
- Cut polenta into circles with a small biscuit cutter. Place a scallop on each circle. Top with sauce.
- This can also be served as an hors d'oeuvres.

Chanterelle Oyster Sauce

½ stick butter	3 Tbls. lemon juice
¼ cup flour	½ pound Chanterelles, sliced
1 cup cream	1 pint small oysters

- Melt the butter in a sauce pan. Stir in flour and cream until thickened. Add other ingredients until oysters are just warmed.

159

SCALLOP AND ASPARAGUS RISOTTO

Serves 4-6

2 Tbls. butter
3 cloves garlic, crushed
2 green onions, chopped
2 cups risotto
3 cups chicken broth
½ cup dry white wine

2 pounds bay scallops
1 pound asparagus, cut in 2"
pieces
Salt and pepper
Grated Romano cheese
Fresh basil leaves

- In a large sauce pan melt the butter. Add the garlic and onions and stir for 2 minutes. Stir in the risotto. Slowly pour in the broth, ½ cup at a time until the risotto begins to thicken.
- In a skillet heat the white wine and stir in the scallops and asparagus for 2 minutes.
- Pour the wine, scallops and asparagus in with the risotto. Season with salt and pepper.
- Place in a serving bowl. Serve with grated cheese and basil leaves.

SCALLOPS WITH FETTUCCINE

Serves 4

½ stick butter
1½ pound bay or sea scallops
1 pound fettuccine
1 pound arugula
1 red onion, sliced

½ pound baby portabella
mushrooms, sliced
½ pound dried tomatoes
2 shallots, minced
¼ cup lemon juice
¼ cup parsley, chopped

- Cook the fettuccine according to directions. Drain
- Melt the butter and sauté scallops until just browned on each side.
- In a large pasta bowl combine all the ingredients.
- Serve as is or with grated cheese.

LINGUINE WITH CLAM SAUCE

Serves 4

24 quahaugs
¼ cup olive oil
1 medium red onion, chopped
1 red bell pepper, chopped
3 cloves garlic, minced
½ pound sun-dried tomatoes

¼ cup parsley
½ teaspoon oregano
1 teaspoon fresh ground pepper
½ teaspoon salt
1 pound linguine
Grated parmesan cheese

- ◆ Preheat oven to 350°
- ◆ Place the clams on a cookie sheet and bake until clams open. Remove shells and chop clams.
- ◆ Heat olive oil in a skillet. Stir in onion and pepper for 4 minutes. Add garlic, sun-dried tomatoes, parsley, oregano, pepper and salt. Let simmer until fettuccine is cooked. Add clams.
- ◆ Cook fettuccine according to directions. Drain.
- ◆ Place fettuccine in large pasta bowl or individual bowls. Top with clams and cheese.

SHRIMP WITH PESTO SAUCE

Serves

1½ pounds medium shrimp,
cooked, peeled and deveined
4 scallions, chopped

2 tomatoes, chopped
¼ cup capers
1 pound seashell pasta

- ◆ Cook pasta according to directions. Drain.
- ◆ In a bowl combine shrimp, scallions, tomatoes, pasta and pesto sauce.

Creamy Pesto Sauce

Pesto – p. 31
1 cup cream

- ◆ Combine ingredients in a bowl.

SHRIMP PASTA

Serves 4

¼ cup olive oil
2 green onions, chopped
¼ cup white wine
¼ cup lemon juice
1 teaspoon pepper
¼ teaspoon cayenne

1½ pounds medium shrimp, cooked, peeled and deveined
¼ pound prosciutto
¼ cup Italian parsley, chopped
1 pound linguine

- ◆ Cook linguine according to instructions. Drain.
- ◆ Combine the ingredients in a pasta bowl.

TUNA PASTA

Serves 4

1 pound tagliatelle
2 pounds fresh tuna, cut into 4 pieces
¼ cup olive oil
2 cloves garlic, crushed

4 large tomatoes, peeled and chopped
¼ cup fresh basil
Juice of one lemon
Fresh basil leaves
Salt and fresh ground pepper

- ◆ Grill the tuna until the desired doneness.
- ◆ Cook the pasta according to the directions. Drain water and keep warm in pan.
- ◆ In a sauce pan heat the oil and add the garlic and tomatoes. Cook until the tomatoes are tender. Add the basil and lemon juice. Add salt and pepper to taste.
- ◆ Serve the pasta with the tuna on top. Pour the tomato sauce over the tuna.
- ◆ Serve immediately garnished with fresh basil leaves.
- ◆ This can be served as a one dish meal by cutting the tuna into cubes after it is grilled. Add to tomato sauce and pour over the pasta.
- ◆ Pasta bow ties can be substituted for the tagliatelle.
- ◆ Grilled swordfish or salmon can be substituted for the tuna.

CHICKEN PASTA

Serves 4

4 small grilled boneless chicken breasts, sliced lengthwise
½ pound smoked Gouda, sliced
1 pound angel hair pasta
1 cup roasted peppers (can be store bought or roasted in oven or on grill)

1 cup black olives
2 scallions, chopped
2 avocados, peeled, pitted and sliced
2 Tbls. lemon juice
2 Tbls. olive oil

- ◆ Cook pasta according to directions. Drain.
- ◆ Combine all ingredients in a large pasta bowl.
- ◆ Serve chilled

CHICKEN AND PENNE

Serves 4

½ stick butter
¼ cup flour
1½ cups cream
¼ pound Gorgonzola
2 cloves garlic, minced
1 pound penne
2 large tomatoes, chopped

2 large boneless chicken breasts, grilled and sliced
2 scallions, chopped
½ pound baby spinach
½ pound broccoli florets
½ cup pine nuts

- ◆ Melt the butter in a sauce pan. Stir in flour and cream until just thickened. Add Gorgonzola and garlic.
- ◆ Cook penne according to instructions. Drain.
- ◆ Toss all ingredients in large pasta bowl. Ingredients can also be layered on pasta.
- ◆ Basil can be substituted for Gorgonzola.

CHICKEN ALFREDO

Serves 4

4 cups cooked chicken
1 pound fettuccine
½ stick butter
4 cloves garlic, minced
1 cup cream
16 cherry tomatoes
1 15 oz. can artichoke hearts
1 red pepper, chopped

1 small zucchini, julienne
1 Tbls. tarragon, chopped
1 Tbls. oregano, chopped
1 Tbls. dill, snipped
1 Tbls. basil, chopped
2 Tbls. parsley, chopped
1 cup grated parmesan cheese

- ◆ Cook the fettuccine according to directions. Drain. Using same pan, heat the butter. Stir in garlic and cream. Add rest of ingredients. Do not boil.
- ◆ Serve warm. More cheese can be served with pasta.
- ◆ A variation of this is to use the chicken, pasta and herbs. Instead of the Alfredo sauce combine 1 chopped scallion, ¼ cup olive oil, 3 Tbls. fresh lemon juice and salt.
- ◆ Sun-dried tomatoes can be substituted for the tomatoes.
- ◆ ½ pound baby spinach can be substituted for the artichokes.
- ◆ Penne or other pasta can be substituted for the fettuccine.

CHICKEN AND PESTO WITH PASTA

Serves 4

Pesto – p. 31
2 large grilled boneless chicken
breasts
1 pound fettuccine

1 cup black olives
1 medium red onion, sliced
1 cup grated mozzarella

- ◆ Cook fettuccine according to directions. Drain
- ◆ Combine ingredients in a pasta bowl.

COUSCOUS WITH CURRANTS

Serves 6-8

4 cups chicken broth
½ stick butter
3 cups couscous
1 cup cranberries

½ cup pine nuts
2 scallions, sliced
¼ cup fresh mint

- ♦ Bring the broth and butter to a boil in a sauce pan. Remove from heat. Stir in couscous. Cover.
- ♦ After 5 minutes fluff the couscous. Add the remaining ingredients.
- ♦ Long grain rice, basmati rice or wild rice can be substituted for the couscous.
- ♦ Currants can be substituted for the cranberries, and chopped walnuts for the pine nuts.
- ♦ This can be served hot or chilled.

SMOKED TURKEY WITH CRANBERRIES AND WILD RICE

Serves 6

2 pounds smoked turkey, cut in
bite size pieces
2 cups wild rice
2 cups cranberries
2 cloves garlic, minced

½ red bell pepper, chopped
3 scallions, chopped
1 cup pecans
6 cups chicken stock
¼ cup sugar

- ♦ Preheat oven to 350
- ♦ Combine all ingredients in a 1 ½ quart casserole.
- ♦ Cover and bake for 45 minutes, or until rice is tender.
- ♦ 2 sliced pears and 1 cup leeks can be substituted for the cranberries and green onions.

CURRIED RICE

Serves 6

1 stalk celery, chopped	1 15 oz. can artichoke hearts
3 scallions, chopped	1 Tbls. curry powder
½ green pepper, chopped	3 cups cooked rice
½ red pepper, chopped	Pinch of saffron

♦ Combine all ingredients in a serving dish. Serve warm.

VEGETABLE AND HAM PASTA

Serves 4

1 pound tagliatelle	2 cups half and half
1 stick butter	1 teaspoon pepper
½ pound asparagus, cut in 2" pieces	Pinch of saffron
½ pound snap peas	2 Tbls. dill, snipped
½ pound broccoli florets	1 pound ham, cut in bite size pieces
1 small zucchini, julienne	1 cup Asiago grated cheese
¼ cup flour	

♦ Cook the tagliatelle according to directions. Drain.
♦ Melt the butter in a large sauce pan. Saute vegetables for 3 minutes. Stir in flour and half and half, until thickened. Add pepper, saffron, dill and ham.
♦ Divide the tagliatelle among 4 pasta bowls. Pour ham sauce on top. Garnish with grated cheese and more grated dill.

BREADS, MUFFINS AND COFFEECAKES

Oliver Wendell Holmes described Beacon Street, Boston, as "the sunny street that holds the sifted few".

New England has many historic gristmills. These and windmills were used to grind corn into flour and cornmeal.

The Old Stone Mill in Newport, RI was rumored to have been built by the Vikings. However, the base is that of a colonial mill, and may have been built by the great-grandfather of Benedict Arnold.

The first grist mill in Massachusetts was erected in Watertown in 1631. In 1633 others were built in Boston and Dorchester. The Eastham Mill was built in 1680 in Plymouth, moved to Truro and is presently located in Eastham. The mill is the oldest on Cape Cod. A restoration of the Old East Mill built in Orleans in 1800 is now located at Heritage Plantation in Sandwich. The Dexter Mill in Sandwich operated from the 1850s until the 19th c. The mill was built on Shawme Pond, an artificial lake built by the early settlers for powering the mill. The Aptucxet Trading Post in Bourne, MA is a recreation of the post established in 1627. On the grounds are a salt works and gristmill.

Five mills were built on Nantucket. The Old Mill was built c1746. The mill is still in operation. On July 10, 1883 Nathan Chapman was granted a patent for a bread cutter, patent 280,796. He owned the Veranda House, later The Overlook Hotel. Tuckernuck Island, just off Nantucket, is an Indian word meaning "Loaf of Bread". The island was originally connected to Nantucket and farmed.

The gristmill c1800 in Guilford, CT and the Old Towne Mill, New London built in 1650 were constructed by John Winthrop, Jr. The Gurleyville Gristmill, Gurleyville was built in the 1830s. The stone mill is one of the last of its kind in New England. The 19th c Bronson Windmill, Fairfield is an unusual eighty foot octagonal tower.

The Perkins Tide Mill, Kennebunkport, ME was built in 1749 and was powered by tidal waters. The mill shut down in 1939 and is now a restaurant.

The Old Adams Grist Mill, Bellows Falls, VT was built in 1831, and was water-powered until 1926. The mill ceased operations in 1956, but is now open to the public. The Old Red Mill, Jericho was built in 1856, shut down at the turn of the century, and is now a museum.

In 1792 the first cracker bakery was opened in Newburyport, MA by baker Theodore Pearson whose first product was pilot's bread, otherwise known as ship's biscuits. Josiah Dent introduced the first biscuits to be called crackers in 1801 in Milton, MA. The biscuits were made of unsweetened and unleavened dough that was rolled many times to make them crisper.

Harry Lender, originally from Lodz, Poland and then New York founded Lender's Bagel Bakery in West Haven, CT in 1926. His sons Murray and Marvin took over the business which still thrives today.

In 1937 Maggie Rudkin began baking Pepperidge Farm Bread at her Connecticut farm. By 1947 the business had grown so rapidly a commercial bakery was opened in Norwalk. Her cookie line was introduced in 1955 and included Bordeaux, Lido, Milano, and Orleans. In 1963 she published "The Margaret Rudkin Pepperidge Farm Cookbook".

Paul (Dean) and Betty Arnold found the Arnold Bread Company in 1940 in Stamford, CT. In 1942 they received a $1500 loan, moved to Port Chester, NY and moved to the present site in Greenwich, CT in the 1960s. Other products include English muffins, Raisin Tea loaf, biscuits, rolls and other breads.

In 1945 Maine and New Hampshire, plus several other states enacted bread enrichment laws.

In 1950 Robert M. Rosenberg opened The Open Kettle in Quincy, MA. This was later to become Dunkin' Donuts.

Au Bon Pan was bought in 1978 by Louis Kane of Boston. In 1981 he and partner Ronald Shaich formed the Au Bon Pain Co., Inc. that had three bakery shops and the Original Cookie Co. The first bakery cart opened at Logan Airport in 1982. In 1984 the chain became a French bakery-café.

SQUASH MUFFINS

1 stick butter
½ cup brown sugar
¼ cup molasses
1 egg
1 cup cooked and mashed squash

1¾ cups flour
1 teaspoon baking soda
½ teaspoon salt
½ cup pecans

- ♦ Preheat oven to 350°
- ♦ In a bowl cream the butter, brown sugar and molasses. Add the other ingredients.
- ♦ Pour into greased muffin tins. Bake 30 minutes or until a toothpick comes out clean.
- ♦ Pumpkin can be substituted for the squash.

SWEET POTATO BISCUITS

1¼ cups flour
1 Tbls. baking powder
1 teaspoon salt
2 Tbls. brown sugar

¾ cup mashed sweet potatoes
¾ cup milk
½ stick butter

- ◆ Preheat oven to 425°.
- ◆ Combine all the ingredients in a food processor.
- ◆ On a floured board roll the dough ½" thick. Use a biscuit cutter to cut the dough into biscuits.
- ◆ Place on an ungreased cookie sheet. Bake for 15 minutes or until just browned.

PUMPKIN BREAD

Makes 1 loaf

2 cups flour
1½ cups sugar
1 teaspoon baking soda
½ teaspoon salt
1 cup pumpkin
1 teaspoon cinnamon
½ teaspoon nutmeg

1 teaspoon allspice
½ teaspoon ground cloves
½ teaspoon ginger
½ cup chopped dates
½ cup pecans
½ cup applesauce
2 eggs

- ◆ Preheat oven to 350°.
- ◆ Combine the ingredients in a bowl and pour into a greased loaf pan.
- ◆ Bake 1 hour.
- ◆ This is good served with cream cheese.

CRANBERRY BREAD

Makes 2 loaves

3 cups cranberries
3 cups sugar
1 cup orange juice
3 eggs, beaten
1½ sticks butter, melted
6 cups flour

3 teaspoons baking powder
1 teaspoon cinnamon
1 teaspoon ginger
½ teaspoon cloves
½ teaspoon nutmeg
1½ cups walnuts or pecans

- In a bowl combine the cranberries, sugar, and orange juice.
- Add the other ingredients. Pour into loaf pans.
- Bake at 350° for one hour.

APPLE CRANBERRY MUFFINS

1 stick butter
1 cup sugar
2 eggs
1 cup orange juice
1 ½ teaspoons baking powder
1 ½ cups flour
Zest of 1 orange
1 teaspoon cinnamon
½ teaspoon grated nutmeg

½ teaspoon allspice
½ teaspoon ginger
½ teaspoon cloves
1 teaspoon almond extract
2 large apples, peeled, cored, and chopped
1 cup fresh cranberries
½ cup walnuts or pecans

- Preheat the oven to 350°.
- In a bowl cream the butter and sugar. Add the eggs and orange. Stir in the flour, baking powder and spices. Stir in the apples, cranberries and nuts.
- Grease 12 muffin cups. Pour in the batter ¾ full. More muffin cups may be needed, depending on size.
- Back 25-30 minutes, or until when pricked with a toothpick the toothpick comes clean.
- Serve with butter, cream cheese, or dust with powdered sugar.
- Milk can be substituted for the orange juice.
- Pears or peaches can be used instead of apples.

CRANBERRY ORANGE MUFFINS

1 stick butter
1 cup sugar
1½ cups flour
2 teaspoons baking powder
2 eggs

½ cup sour cream
½ cup orange juice
1 cup fresh cranberries
Zest of 1 orange

- ♦ Preheat oven to 350°
- ♦ Cream the butter in a bowl. Add sugar. Beat in rest of ingredients.
- ♦ Bake 30 minutes, or until toothpick comes out clean.

APPLE PECAN MUFFINS

Makes 12 muffins

1 stick butter
½ cup sugar
½ cup brown sugar
1½ cups flour
2 teaspoons baking powder
2 eggs
Zest of 1 orange
½ cup orange juice

½ teaspoon cloves
1 teaspoon cinnamon
½ teaspoon ginger
½ teaspoon nutmeg
2 apples, peeled, cored and diced
1 cup pecans

- ♦ Preheat oven to 350°.
- ♦ In a mixing bowl cream the butter and sugars. Add the rest of the ingredients.
- ♦ Pour into greased muffin tins.
- ♦ Bake ½ hour or until a toothpick comes out clean.
- ♦ Serve warm with cream cheese or butter.

CHEDDAR APPLE BISCUITS

2 cups flour
1 Tbls. baking powder
6 Tbls. butter

¼ pound cheddar cheese
¾ cup half and half
1 apple, peeled and cored

- ♦ Preheat oven to 425°
- ♦ In a food processor combine all ingredients until a ball is formed. Roll out the dough on a floured board. Cut with a biscuit cutter.
- ♦ Place on an ungreased cookie sheet.
- ♦ Bake for 12-15 minutes, or until just browned.

APPLESAUCE BREAD OR MUFFINS

Makes 1 loaf

1 stick butter
1 cup sugar
1 egg
1 teaspoon baking soda
1 teaspoon vanilla

1 ½ cups flour
½ teaspoon allspice
1 teaspoon cinnamon
1 cup pecans
1 cup applesauce

- ♦ Preheat oven to 350°
- ♦ In a bowl cream the butter and sugar. Add the other ingredients. Pour into a greased bread loaf pan or muffin tins.
- ♦ Bake 30 minutes or until a toothpick comes out clean.
- ♦ Serve with cream cheese.

COCONUT COFFEE CAKE

1 stick butter
1 cup sugar
1½ cups flour
2 eggs
1 cup sour cream

1 teaspoon almond flavoring
Zest of 1 lemon
½ cup grated coconut
½ cup pecans

- ♦ Preheat oven to 350°
- ♦ Cream the butter and sugar in a bowl. Beat in other ingredients.
- ♦ Pour into greased baking dish. Spread topping.
- ♦ Bake 45 minutes.

Topping

¼ cup brown sugar
¼ cup sugar

1 teaspoon cinnamon
½ cup pecans

- ♦ Combine ingredients in a bowl.

RAISIN BANANA BREAD

1 stick butter
1 cup sugar
2 eggs
2 cups flour
1½ teaspoons baking powder

¼ cup milk
Juice of ½ lemon
2 bananas, peeled and mashed
1 cup seedless raisins

- ♦ Preheat oven to 350°
- ♦ In a bowl cream the butter and sugar. Add other ingredients.
- ♦ Pour batter into 2 loaf pans.
- ♦ Bake 45 minutes or until toothpick comes clean.
- ♦ 2 large chopped apples can replace the bananas.

ORANGE BREAD

3 cups flour
4 teaspoons baking powder
½ teaspoon salt
1 cup sugar

1 egg
¼ cup grated orange rind
1 cup orange juice
1 stick butter, melted

- Preheat oven to 350°
- Combine all ingredients in a bowl.
- Bake in 2 loaf pans for 1 hour

CANDIED FRUIT COFFEE CAKE

This is very pretty for Christmas

1 stick butter
1 cup sugar
2 eggs
1½ cups flour

1 cup sour cream
1½ teaspoons baking powder
1 cup mixed candied fruits
1 cup pecans or walnuts

- Preheat oven to 350°
- Cream the butter and sugar. Add other ingredients.
- Pour into greased 13 x 9 baking dish. Pour topping over batter
- Bake 45 minutes.

Topping

1 Tbls. cinnamon
¼ cup sugar

¼ brown sugar

- Combine ingredients in bowl.

Instead of topping you can use this icing instead:

1 cup powdered sugar
½ stick butter

2 Tbls. cream
½ teaspoon vanilla

- Beat ingredients in a bowl.
- Drizzle over coffee cake while still warm.

BUTTERSCOTCH COFFEE CAKE

2¼ cups flour   1 stick butter
3 teaspoons baking powder   ¾ cup milk
½ teaspoon salt   2 eggs
1 cup brown sugar

- ♦ Preheat oven to 375°
- ♦ Combine ingredients in a bowl.
- ♦ Pour into greased baking dish.
- ♦ Spread topping over batter.
- ♦ Bake 30-35 minutes, or until toothpick comes out clean.

Topping

1 Tbls. cinnamon
½ cup brown sugar
½ teaspoon nutmeg

- ♦ Combine all ingredients in bowl.

PEAR NUT BREAD

1 stick butter   Zest of 1 lemon
1 cup sugar   Juice of ½ lemon
2 cups flour   1 cup walnuts
2 eggs   3 pears, peeled, seeded and
2 teaspoons baking powder   chopped
½ cup sour cream

- ♦ Preheat oven to 350°
- ♦ Cream the sugar and butter. Add other ingredients.
- ♦ Pour into 2 loaf pans.
- ♦ Bake 40 minutes

RASPBERRY MUFFINS

Makes 1 dozen

1 stick butter
½ cup sugar
½ cup brown sugar
1 egg
1 ½ cups flour

2 teaspoons baking powder
1 cup sour cream
1 teaspoon cinnamon
½ teaspoon vanilla
1 cup fresh raspberries

- ◆ Preheat oven to 350°.
- ◆ In a mixing bowl combine the butter and sugars. Stir in the egg, flour, baking powder, sour cream, cinnamon and vanilla. Gently fold in the raspberries.
- ◆ Butter 12 muffin cups. Add batter. Sprinkle with topping.
- ◆ Bake 25 minutes or until just browned and a toothpick comes out dry.
- ◆ Blueberries, peaches or other fruit can be substituted for the raspberries.

Topping

½ stick butter
¼ cup sugar
½ cup brown sugar

½ cup pecans
1 teaspoon cinnamon

- ◆ In a sauce pan melt the butter. Remove from heat and stir in the other ingredients.

WALNUT BREAD

1 stick butter
1 cup sugar
2 eggs
1 ½ cups flour
1 cup sour cream

2 teaspoons baking powder
¼ cup cocoa
¼ cup ground coffee
1 teaspoon cinnamon
1 cup walnuts

- ◆ Preheat oven to 350°
- ◆ Cream the butter and sugar. Add other ingredients.
- ◆ Pour into greased baking dish
- ◆ Bake 45 minutes, or until toothpick comes out clean.

PEACH COFFEE CAKE

1 stick butter
1 cup sugar
2 eggs
1 cup sour cream
1½ teaspoons baking powder
1½ cups flour
1 teaspoon vanilla
2 large peaches, peeled, pitted
and sliced

1 cup pecans
¼ cup white sugar
¼ cup dark brown sugar
1 Tbls. cinnamon

- ◆ Preheat oven to 350°.
- ◆ In a bowl beat the butter, sugar, eggs, sour cream, baking powder, flour and vanilla, and peaches.
- ◆ Pour the batter in a 9" x 13" glass baking dish.
- ◆ In a small bowl combine the pecans, sugars and cinnamon. Pour over the batter.
- ◆ Bake 40 minutes or until a toothpick comes out clean.
- ◆ Apples, pears or blueberries can be substituted for the peaches.

LILI'S DROP DONUT BALLS

½ cup sugar
½ cup milk
1 egg
1½ cups flour
2 teaspoons baking powder

½ teaspoon cinnamon
½ teaspoon salt
½ teaspoon nutmeg
Powdered sugar
Vegetable oil

- ◆ In a bowl combine all the ingredients except the powdered sugar and oil.
- ◆ Heat a skillet with the vegetable oil. Drop the dough by teaspoons. Fry until just browned.
- ◆ Roll in powdered sugar.

RHUBARB BREAD

Makes 1 loaf

1 cup rhubarb, diced
¼ cup sugar
3 cups flour
1 Tbls. baking powder
1 cup sugar
2 Tbls. orange zest
½ cup walnuts

¾ cup milk
1 egg
½ stick butter
¼ cup orange juice

- ◆ Preheat oven to 350°
- ◆ In a bowl combine all the ingredients. Pour into a greased bread loaf pan.
- ◆ Bake 1 hour.

ZUCCHINI BREAD

Makes 2 loaves

¾ cup vegetable oil
1½ cups sugar
3 eggs
3 cups flour
1 teaspoon baking powder
1 teaspoon baking soda
1 teaspoon cinnamon

½ teaspoon nutmeg
½ teaspoon ginger
½ teaspoon cloves
Zest of 1 orange
2 cups zucchini, grated
½ cup pecans

- ◆ Preheat oven to 350°
- ◆ In a bowl combine the vegetable oil and zucchini. Add the rest of the ingredients.
- ◆ Pour into 2 greased bread loaf pans.
- ◆ Bake for 1 hour.

DATE NUT MUFFINS

Makes 12 muffins

1 stick butter
1 cup sugar
1½ cups flour
2 eggs
2 teaspoons baking powder
½ cup dates
½ cup pecans

½ cup coconut
2 apples, peeled, cored and
diced
½ cup carrots, grated
Zest of 1 lemon
¼ cup brandy

- ♦ Preheat oven to 350°
- ♦ Cream the butter and sugar in a bowl. Add the other ingredients.
- ♦ Pour into greased muffin tins.
- ♦ Bake 35 minutes.
- ♦ 1 teaspoon cinnamon can be substituted for the lemon zest.

BLUEBERRY BANANA BREAD

1 stick butter
1 cup sugar
2 eggs
1½ cups flour
2 teaspoons baking powder

1 teaspoon vanilla
¼ cup orange juice
1 cup fresh blueberries
2 bananas mashed

- ♦ Preheat oven to 350°
- ♦ Cream butter and sugar. Add eggs, flour, baking powder, vanilla and orange juice. Fold in blueberries and bananas.
- ♦ Pour batter into loaf pan
- ♦ Bake for 1 hour.

BLUEBERRY BREAD

Makes 1 loaf

1 stick butter
1 cup sugar
1½ cups flour
2 eggs
1 teaspoon vanilla

2 teaspoons baking powder
Zest of 1 orange
1 cup orange juice
2 cups blueberries
½ cup pecans

- ◆ Preheat oven to 350°
- ◆ In a bowl cream the butter and sugar. Add the flour, eggs, vanilla, baking powder, orange zest and orange juice. Fold in the blueberries and pecans.
- ◆ Pour into a greased bread loaf pan.
- ◆ Bake for 1 hour.
- ◆ A variation of this is to use only 1 cup blueberries, 1 cup applesauce, 1 teaspoon cinnamon, and 8 dried apricots, chopped.

ROSEMARY PARMESAN BREAD

Makes 1 loaf

1 cup warm water
1 package yeast
2 Tbls. olive oil
1 teaspoon kosher salt

3 cups flour
½ cup fresh grated parmesan cheese
¼ cup fresh rosemary

- ◆ Preheat oven to
- ◆ In a food processor combine all ingredients until a ball is formed.
- ◆ Place in a greased bowl. Let rise 1 hour.
- ◆ Place on a cookie sheet and shape into a loaf. Let rise 1 hour.
- ◆ Heat oven to 500°.
- ◆ Bake for 15 minutes or until golden in color.
- ◆ Dill can be substituted for the rosemary.

EGG AND BRUNCH DISHES

The fishing fleet in New Bedford has dwindled in size, but fishing boats still call the historic whaling town home.

The Abenaki tribe first taught the colonists how to tap the maple sugar trees, making a gash in the tree, and collecting the sap. The maple sugaring season begins in mid-February and usually finishes up in April. Almost forty gallons of sap are needed to make one gallon of maple syrup. "Boiling down" is done at a sugar house, many of which are open to the public. The New England Maple Museum, Pittsford, the Maple Grove Maple Museum, St. Johnsbury, and the Old Colony Maple Sugar Factory, Newport, have exhibits on maple sugaring.

Vermont also produces excellent dairy products such as Cabot Cheese, which is a cooperative founded in 1919.

Christopher and Rebecca Gore built Gore Place in Waltham, MA in 1806. Mr. Gore served as Massachusetts governor and United States Senator. The first floor of the house was designed for entertaining and the Gore's once entertained 450 for breakfast!

Timothy Earle of Smithfield, RI was granted a patent for an egg beater with a rack-and-pinion movement in 1863.

John F. Blondell of Thomaston, ME patented a doughnut cutter in 1872.

LOBSTER QUICHE

Serves 4

1 pie crust
½ pound lobster meat
1 cup leeks, chopped
¼ cup dill
1 cup Gruyere, grated

2½ cups half and half
3 eggs
2 Tbls. lemon juice

- ◆ Preheat oven to 400°
- ◆ Place the lobster, leeks, dill and Gruyere in pie crust.
- ◆ In a bowl beat the eggs, half and half and lemon juice. Pour over the lobster mixture.
- ◆ Bake for 45 minutes, or until just browned.
- ◆ Salmon, crab or other seafood can be substituted for the lobster.

LOBSTER CREPES

Serves 10, 2 crepes each

2 sticks butter	1 pound mushrooms, sliced
1 cup flour	1 pound baby spinach
4 cups half and half	½ cup fresh basil
½ cup Sherry	Salt and pepper to taste
½ stick butter	2 pounds lobster meat

- ◆ Preheat oven to 325°
- ◆ Melt 1½ sticks butter in a sauce pan. Add flour and stir in half and half until thickened. Stir in Sherry.
- ◆ In a skillet melt the ½ stick butter. Add mushrooms and spinach and just lightly saute. Add basil, salt and pepper. Stir into white sauce.
- ◆ Spread lobster meat evenly in middle of each crepe. Pour some of sauce over lobster. Roll crepe. Place on baking dish.
- ◆ Bake for 15 minutes or until just warmed.
- ◆ Remove from oven. Serve on plates with warm mushroom sauce.
- ◆ Ham, chicken or crab can be substituted for the lobster.

Crepes

Makes about 20

4 eggs	2 cups flour
2 cups milk	¼ cup chives, snipped
6 Tbls. butter, melted	

- ◆ Combine the ingredients in a bowl.
- ◆ Heat a crepe pan or small skillet. Add a dollop of butter.
- ◆ Spoon about 2 Tbls. batter into pan, turning pan so that batter is spread evenly. Brown for about 1 minute on each side.

LOBSTER OMELET

Serves 4

8 eggs
½ stick butter
½ pound lobster meat

1 cup leeks, chopped
½ cup Gruyere
¼ cup dill

- ♦ Beat the eggs in a bowl.
- ♦ Melt the butter in a large skillet. Add eggs. Scrape sides of pan to keep from sticking.
- ♦ When eggs are just about set sprinkle other ingredients on top. Cook several more minutes.
- ♦ Carefully slid the omelet out of pan and fold over in half.
- ♦ Cut into 4 slices. Serve on plates and garnish with lemon slices and dill.

VEGETABLE FRITTATA

Serves 4

½ stick butter
8 eggs
½ pound asparagus, cut in 1" pieces
½ pound baby portabella mushrooms, sliced

½ red bell pepper, chopped
½ yellow pepper, chopped
2 green onions, chopped
2 cooked red bliss potatoes, diced
¼ cup dill

- ♦ Preheat oven to 400°
- ♦ Beat the eggs in a bowl.
- ♦ Melt the butter in an iron skillet. Pour the eggs into skillet. Scrape sides to keep from sticking. Cook for 4 minutes. Add vegetables.
- ♦ Put in oven for about 10-15 minutes, until eggs are set.
- ♦ Grated cheddar, Monterrey Jack cheese or sour cream can be added.
- ♦ Vegetables such as broccoli, zucchini or squash can be added or substituted.

ASPARAGUS STRATA

This can be used as a side dish or for a brunch.

Serves 10-12

½ stick butter
2 medium onions, chopped
3 pounds asparagus, cut into 1"
slices
1 cup dry bread crumbs
¼ cup fresh dill, chopped
Salt and pepper

6 hard boiled eggs, sliced
1 pound sharp cheddar cheese,
grated
8 eggs, beaten

- ◆ Preheat oven to 350°.
- ◆ In a large iron skillet melt the butter and add the onions and asparagus, cooking until just tender. Stir in the breadcrumbs, dill, salt and pepper to taste.
- ◆ Place the hard boiled eggs on the asparagus mixture. Sprinkle with the cheese.
- ◆ Pour the beaten eggs over the whole mixture.
- ◆ Place in oven and bake for 15-20 minutes until the eggs are set.

SCRAMBLED EGGS DELUXE

Serves 4

½ stick butter
8 eggs
8 slices maple smoked bacon
2 tomatoes, chopped

2 green onions, chopped
½ pound cheddar cheese, grated
½ cup sour cream

- ◆ Melt the butter in a skillet.
- ◆ Beat eggs in a bowl. Pour into the skillet. Scrape sides to keep from sticking. Add other ingredients.
- ◆ Cook and stir until eggs are just firm.
- ◆ To make an omelet, add other ingredients just before eggs become firm. Slide from pan onto plate and fold in half. Cut into 4 slices.

SCRAMBLED EGGS WITH LINGUICA

Serves 4

½ stick butter
8 eggs
½ pound linguica, sliced
2 tomatoes, chopped

½ pound baby spinach
4 cloves garlic, minced
2 green onions, chopped

- ♦ Melt butter in a skillet.
- ♦ Beat eggs in a bowl. Stir into butter. Add other ingredients. Cook until eggs are set.
- ♦ Serve garnished with sour cream and cilantro or parsley.

SEAFOOD AND MEAT FRITTATA

Serves 4

¼ cup olive oil
4 red bliss potatoes, sliced
1 medium onion, sliced
½ pound fresh peas
½ pound ham, diced

½ pound small shrimp
½ pound chorizo, sliced
8 eggs
Salt and pepper
¼ cup fresh basil or oregano

- ♦ Preheat oven to 350°
- ♦ In a large iron skillet melt the butter and add the potatoes and onions. Saute until tender. Add the peas. Stir in the ham, shrimp, chorizo, salt and pepper.
- ♦ Beat the eggs in a bowl. Pour into the skillet. Turn up heat until just bubbling.
- ♦ Place in oven for about 10-15 minutes, until set.
- ♦ Serve garnished with basil or oregano.

CHORIZO FRITTATA

Serves 4

2 Tbls. olive oil
2 scallions, chopped
¼ cup red pepper, chopped
¼ cup green pepper, chopped
1 jalapeno, seeded and chopped
12 black olives, sliced
1 large tomato, sliced

1 pound chorizo, sliced
1 cup mozzarella cheese, grated
8 eggs
1 teaspoon chili powder
Salt and pepper
Cilantro

♦ Preheat the oven to 350°.
♦ Heat the olive oil in a large iron skillet and add the scallions and peppers. Saute for 5 minutes or until just tender. Add the olives, tomatoes, chorizo and cheese.
♦ In a bowl beat the eggs with the chili powder and salt and pepper. Pour over the vegetable, chorizo mixture. Heat once more on the stove until just bubbling.
♦ Place in oven for 20 minutes or until set.
♦ Remove from heat and serve in slices. Garnish with cilantro leaves.

EGGS BENEDICT

Serves 4

4 English muffins, split and toasted
8 hard boiled eggs, sliced

1 large tomato, thinly sliced
½ pound crab meat

♦ Place 1 sliced tomato and divide crab and egg among the 8 muffins. Top with Hollandaise.

Spinach Hollandaise

♦ Make Hollandaise according to directions – p. 206, but add ¼ pound baby spinach to food processor. Blend until smooth.

PANCAKES & BLUEBERRY SAUCE

Makes about 8 small pancakes.

1 cup flour	1 egg
¼ teaspoon salt	1 cup milk
¼ cup sugar	¼ cup sour cream
1 tablespoon baking powder	2 tablespoons melted butter

- In bowl beat egg, milk and sour cream. Add salt, sugar, baking powder, flour, then butter.
- Pour the batter by large spoonfuls into a skillet and cook about 4 minutes to a side.
- Serve with blueberry sauce or maple syrup and butter.

Blueberry and Peach Sauce

2 Tbls. sugar	1 cup blueberries
1 Tbls. corn starch	1 large peach, peeled, pitted and
½ cup water	chopped
Juice of ½ lemon	

- Heat the sugar, cornstarch, water and lemon juice in a sauce pan. Bring to a boil. Stir in the blueberries and peaches. Serve warm.
- Raspberries or blackberries can be substituted for blueberries.

CORN PANCAKES

Serves 4

2 cups fresh corn	½ teaspoon salt
½ cup cornmeal	1 cup milk
½ cup flour	2 Tbls. butter
1 teaspoon baking powder	2 Tbls. sour cream
¼ cup sugar	2 eggs, separated

- In a bowl combine the corn, cornmeal, flour, baking powder, sugar, salt, egg yolks, milk butter and sour cream.
- In a separate bowl beat the egg whites. Fold into the dough.
- Heat a greased griddle and drop dough by large spoonfuls, turning once.
- Serve with syrup, honey, molasses or blueberry syrup

CREAMED FINNAN HADDIE

Finnan haddie is smoked haddock.

Serves 4

1 stick butter	1 teaspoon dry mustard
½ cup flour	¼ teaspoon cayenne
2 cups half and half	½ teaspoon paprika
½ red bell pepper, chopped	1 teaspoon Worcestershire
½ yellow pepper, chopped	2 Tbls. Sherry
2 pounds finnan haddie, broken up into small pieces	4 English muffins or 2 cups cooked rice

- ◆ In a saucepan melt the butter. Stir in the flour and slowly add the half and half until thickened.
- ◆ Add peppers, finnan haddie, mustard, cayenne, paprika, Worcestershire and Sherry.
- ◆ Serve on toasted English muffins, or rice.
- ◆ Dried codfish can be substituted for the finnan haddie.

POLENTA

Serves 4

1 cup cornmeal	½ cup parmesan, Swiss or Monterrey Jack cheese
2 cups water	
2 Tbls. butter	

- ◆ Preheat oven to 350°
- ◆ Bring water to boil in sauce pan. Add cornmeal. Stir until thickened. Stir in butter and cheese.
- ◆ Pour into greased square baking dish.
- ◆ Bake 15-20 minutes, just browned. Cut in slices.
- ◆ Butter can also be melted in baking dish and just pour polenta into that and bake.

SANDWICHES AND PIZZA

Table set for an elegant ladies' tea

Frank Pepe's Pizzeria Napoletana, New Haven, CT claims to have created the first pizza in the United States in 1925. The coal-fired oven is still used.

Louis' Lunch, New Haven, CT also claims to have served a first – that the first hamburger sandwiches were created here in 1900.

The Mystic Pizza, Mystic, CT provided the back drop for the movie of the same name in 1988.

LOBSTER TACO WITH SALSA

Serves 4

1 pound lobster meat
1 cup jalapeno Monterrey jack cheese, shredded

1 cup baby spinach leaves
4 tortillas

- ♦ Preheat oven to 350°.
- ♦ Place the tortillas on a cookie sheet. Heat the tortillas until just warmed.
- ♦ Combine the lobster meat, cheese and spinach in a bowl.
- ♦ Place the tortillas on individual plates. Down the center of each tortilla spoon the lobster mixture. Roll up. Garnish with salsa and lemon slice.

Salsa

2 large tomatoes, finely chopped
1 cup corn
2 cloves garlic, crushed
¼ cup cilantro, chopped
1 Tbls. white wine vinegar
1 Tbls. olive oil

2 jalapenos, seeded and chopped
Juice of 1 lime

- ♦ In a bowl combine the ingredients

SEAFOOD BURRITO

Serves 4-6

½ pound smoked salmon
1 pound crab meat
¼ cup fresh basil, chopped

Lobster cream sauce – p. 68
Wheat tortillas

- ◆ Preheat oven to 400°
- ◆ Place a small amount of salmon and crab down center of tortilla. Add some of the cream sauce. Fold tortilla around mixture. Place in baking dish. Do this with each tortilla. Spoon rest of sauce on top.
- ◆ Bake 10 minutes or until just bubbling.
- ◆ Serve with rice, black beans, sour cream, and guacamole.

VEGETARIAN BURRITO

4 burritos

1 red bell pepper, sliced
1 green pepper, sliced
4 jalapeno, sliced lengthwise
and seeds removed
2 medium red onions, sliced
4 tomatoes, sliced

1 15 oz. can black beans,
drained
2 cups Monterey Jack cheese,
grated
4 wheat tortillas

- ◆ Place the peppers, jalapeno, onions and tomatoes in a grill basket. Grill until just tender.
- ◆ They can also be baked on a cookie sheet in a 400° for ½ hour.
- ◆ Divide up the ingredients between the 4 burritos.
- ◆ They can be warmed up on a cookie sheet in the oven or served cold with salsa, guacamole and sour cream.

VEGETARIAN QUESADILLA

Serves 6

4 large tomatoes, finely chopped
2 red onions, chopped
1 pound fresh baby spinach, chopped
1 15 oz. can black beans

¼ cup cilantro, chopped
8 ounces cream cheese
½ pound grated cheddar cheese
12 10" tortillas

- ♦ Preheat oven to 400°
- ♦ In a bowl combine all the ingredients, except tortillas.
- ♦ Spread mixture on 6 tortillas. Top with other tortillas.
- ♦ Place on a baking sheet.
- ♦ Bake 10 minutes or until bubbling.
- ♦ Serve with guacamole and sour cream.

CHEESE PIZZA

Dough – p. 195
1 cup fresh grated parmesan cheese
1 cup mozzarella, grated
1 cup Asiago cheese, grated
½ pound pancetta, cut in pieces

¼ cup basil, chopped
2 Tbls. oregano, chopped
2 Tbls. rosemary, chopped
2 Tbls. olive oil

- ♦ Preheat oven to 425°
- ♦ Spread the cheeses on the crust.
- ♦ Add pancetta and herbs. Drizzle the olive oil on top.
- ♦ Bake 15-20 minutes, or until bubbling.

VEGETARIAN PIZZA

Serves 4

Dough

3½ cups flour
1 package yeast
1 cup lukewarm water

1 teaspoon kosher salt
1 Tbls. olive oil

- ◆ Dissolve the yeast in the water.
- ◆ Place ingredients in food processor until ball form.
- ◆ Let rise in oiled bowl, covered for 1 hour.
- ◆ Roll out dough in shape of pizza pan.

2 large tomatoes, thinly sliced
1 cup fresh baby spinach
½ pound mushrooms, sliced
1 scallion, sliced
2 cloves garlic, crushed

½ cup fresh basil
2 Tbls. fresh oregano
2 Tbls. olive oil
½ pound Gruyere cheese, grated

- ◆ Preheat oven to 425°
- ◆ Arrange the tomatoes in a layer on the dough.
- ◆ Top with spinach, mushrooms, scallion, garlic, basil and oregano. Dribble the olive oil over the vegetables.
- ◆ Top with the Gruyere.
- ◆ Bake for 15-20 minutes or until bubbling and the crust is golden.

LOBSTER PIZZA

Dough- See above
2 large tomatoes, sliced thinly
1 yellow pepper, sliced thinly
1 red pepper, sliced thinly

½ pound shitake mushrooms, sliced
½ pound lobster meat
½ pound Gruyere, grated

- ◆ Preheat oven to 425°
- ◆ Arrange the tomatoes first on pizza dough. Then top with peppers, mushrooms, lobster and finally Gruyere.
- ◆ Bake 15-20 minutes or until bubbling.
- ◆ Mussels, scallops, crab or other seafood can be substituted.

TOMATO AND PESTO PIZZA

Serves

Dough- p. 195
Pesto – p. (double recipe)
4 large tomatoes, sliced thinly

2 cups fresh grated parmesan cheese

- ◆ Preheat oven to 425°
- ◆ Arrange the tomatoes on pizza dough. Top with pesto and then cheese.
- ◆ Bake 15-20 minutes or until bubbling.

TOMATO AND SPINACH PIZZA

Dough- p.195
4 large tomatoes, sliced thinly
½ pound pepperoni, sliced
1 green pepper, sliced thinly
1 red bell pepper, sliced thinly
½ pound baby spinach
4 cloves garlic, minced

¼ cup bail, chopped
2 Tbls. oregano, chopped
1 cup pitted black or Greek olives
2 Tbls. olive oil
2 cups mozzarella, grated

- ◆ Preheat oven to 425°
- ◆ Arrange the tomatoes on the dough.
- ◆ Top with other ingredients, ending with cheese.
- ◆ Bake 15-20 minutes, or until bubbling.
- ◆ Tomatoes can also be pureed with garlic and olive oil, and then spread on dough.

ROAST BEEF SANDWICH

Serves 4

8 slices Portuguese or herb
bread
1 pound roast beef, sliced thinly
1 container boursin cheese

4 lettuce leaves
2 tomatoes, sliced
¼ cup basil, chopped

- ♦ Spread the boursin on each bread slice. Divide up roast beef, tomatoes, lettuce and basil among each sandwich.
- ♦ Blue cheese and grilled onions can be substituted for the boursin.

GRILLED STEAK SANDWICH

Serves 4

1 pound beef tenderloin
2 red onions, sliced
1 green pepper, sliced

1 red pepper, sliced
Portuguese bread or rolls

- ♦ Grill the beef on BBQ until desired pinkness. Slice thinly. Grill onions and peppers in grill basket.
- ♦ Divide the beef, onions and peppers on each slice of bread or roll. Top with dressing.
- ♦ Grilled chopped sirloin burgers or chicken can be substituted for the beef.

Gorgonzola Dressing

½ pound Gorgonzola cheese
¼ cup mayonnaise

¼ cup sour cream
¼ cup basil, chopped

- ♦ Combine all the ingredients in a bowl.

GRILLED CHICKEN SANDWICH

4 sandwiches

2 grilled boneless chicken breasts
¼ cup cilantro, chopped
1 yellow pepper, sliced
1 red pepper, sliced
2 red onions, sliced

4 Boston lettuce, leaves
½ pound Monterrey jack cheese, sliced
½ cup mayonnaise
8 slices Portuguese or herb bread or rolls.

- ♦ Grill the chicken on a BBQ. Slice thinly. Grill peppers and onions in a grill basket.
- ♦ Spread the mayonnaise on the bread. Top with other ingredients.

TURKEY SANDWICH

Serves 4

1 container boursin
1 pound smoked turkey
1 jar cranberry sauce or chutney

4 Boston lettuce leaves
8 slices Portuguese or herb bread

- ♦ Spread the boursin on bread. Top with other ingredients.

TURKEY SANDWICH II

Serves 6

1 pound smoked turkey
½ pound Swiss cheese, sliced
½ pound cheddar cheese, sliced
2 avocadoes, peeled, pitted and sliced

1 cup mayonnaise
6 Boston lettuce leaves
2 tomatoes, sliced
12 slices herb bread

- ♦ Spread the mayonnaise on bread. Top with other ingredients.

VEGETARIAN SANDWICH

Serves 6

1 container boursin cheese
Dijon mustard
2 avocadoes, peeled, pitted and
sliced
1 pint bean sprouts

1 cucumber, sliced
6 Boston lettuce leaves
2 tomatoes, sliced
12 slices Portuguese or herb
bread

- ♦ Spread 6 slices of the bread with the boursin and 6 with mustard.
- ♦ Divide the other ingredients among the sandwiches.

VEGGIE SANDWICH

Serves 4

1 large loaf French or Italian
bread
1 recipe pesto – p. 31
1 large eggplant, sliced
¼ cup olive oil

½ pound mushrooms, sliced
2 red peppers, sliced
1 red onion, sliced thinly
2 tomatoes, sliced
½ pound Mozzarella, sliced

- ♦ Preheat oven to 400°
- ♦ Place the eggplant slices on cookie sheet. Bake ½ hour or until just browned.
- ♦ Slice the bread lengthwise.
- ♦ Spread the pesto on bread and top with other ingredients.
- ♦ Cut into 4 sandwiches, or smaller slices if serving for an hors d'oeuvres.
- ♦ Can also be toasted under broiler until cheese just melts.

BRIE SANDWICH

Serves 4

8 slices Portuguese or herb
bread
1 round brie, sliced
½ pound sun-dried tomatoes
4 Boston lettuce leaves

½ pint bean sprouts
1 cucumber, sliced
1 cup shredded carrots
½ cup mayonnaise

- ♦ Spread the mayonnaise on each slice of bread.
- ♦ Divide up the other ingredients among each sandwich.
- ♦ Can be served open-faced or as sandwich.

BACON SANDWICH

Serves 4

2 red peppers, sliced
½ pound baby spinach

8 slices bacon
8 slices Portuguese bread

- ♦ Roast peppers in grill basket on BBQ or in oven. Can also be store bought.
- ♦ Toast bread. Spread with aioli. Top with peppers, spinach and bacon.

Lemon Aioli

½ cup mayonnaise
¼ cup milk

Juice of 1 lemon
2 cloves garlic, minced

- ♦ Combine ingredients in a bowl.

JAMS, CHUTNEYS AND OTHER CONDIMENTS

Ocean Spray Cranberry Sauce was first produced in 1912. The first cannery was in Hanson, MA.

Fresh Fruit and Sour Cream Dip

CRANBERRY CHUTNEY

Makes 1 dozen jars

4 cups cranberries
½ cup vinegar
1 cup sugar
2 cups water
1 large red onion, chopped
1 cup walnuts

1 cup currants or raisins
¼ pound crystallized ginger, cut in pieces
½ teaspoon cloves
½ teaspoon cayenne

- ♦ In a large pot boil the cranberries, onion, vinegar, sugar and water until thickened.
- ♦ Stir in the walnuts, currants and spices.
- ♦ Sterilize canning jars in a boiling pot of water.
- ♦ Pour the chutney into the jars and cover with melted paraffin, or seal jars.

APPLE CRANBERRY CHUTNEY

Makes approximately 16 8 ounce jars

4 pounds fresh cranberries
4 cups sugar
2 cups dark brown sugar
2 cups currants
2 Tbls. cinnamon
2 Tbls. fresh ginger, grated
1 teaspoon nutmeg

1 teaspoon ground cloves
1 teaspoon allspice
4 cups water
2 large red onions, diced
4 large apples, cored and diced
2 cups pecans

- ♦ Combine all the ingredients in a large kettle. Bring to a boil and cook until cranberries pop.
- ♦ In another kettle bring water to a boil. Drop in jars and tops.
- ♦ Fill jars with hot apple cranberry mixture. Seal jars.

CRANBERRY APPLE CHUTNEY

4 cups cranberries
2 apples, cored, peeled and diced
½ cup vinegar
1 cup sugar
2 cups water
1 large red onion, chopped
1 cup walnuts
1 cup currants or raisins

¼ cup fresh ginger, grated
½ teaspoon cloves
½ teaspoon nutmeg
¼ teaspoon allspice
½ teaspoon cayenne

- ◆ In a large pot boil the cranberries, onion, vinegar, sugar and water until thickened.
- ◆ Stir in the walnuts, currants and spices.
- ◆ Sterilize canning jars in a boiling pot of water.
- ◆ Pour the chutney into the jars and cover with melted paraffin, or seal jars.

TOMATO CHUTNEY

4 large tomatoes
1 cup vinegar
1 large red onion
1 Tbls. cinnamon
1 cup brown sugar

2 Tbls. fresh grated ginger
4 cloves garlic, grated
½ teaspoon cayenne
¼ cup coriander, chopped
2 Tbls. mustard seeds

- ◆ Combine all ingredients in a large sauce pan. Bring to a boil.
- ◆ Simmer until tomatoes are tender and chutney thickens. Remove from heat. Cool.
- ◆ Put in jars and keep refrigerated. Does not keep more than 2-3 weeks.

FRUIT CHUTNEY

4 pounds peaches, peeled, pitted
and chopped finely
4 apples, peeled, pitted and
chopped finely
1 cup cider vinegar
¼ cup lemon juice
1 cup raisins
1 pound brown sugar
½ cup onion, chopped

¼ cup crystallized ginger,
chopped
1 Tbls. salt
1 teaspoon allspice
1 teaspoon cinnamon
½ teaspoon cloves
1 teaspoon ginger
¼ teaspoon cayenne
2 Tbls. mustard seed

- ♦ Combine all ingredients in a large pot. Bring to a boil. Simmer 15 minutes, or peaches are tender. Simmer less time if peaches are very ripe.
- ♦ Sterilize jars in boiling water. Pour chutney into jars. Seal immediately.

FRUIT SAUCE

½ stick butter
1 Tbls. cornstarch
½ cup orange juice
1 cup cashews
2 pears, peeled, cored and
chopped

2 oranges, peeled and sectioned
2 Tbls. fresh grated ginger
2 Tbls. mint, chopped
¼ cup rum

- ♦ Melt butter in a sauce pan. Stir in cornstarch and orange juice until slightly thickened. Add rest of ingredients.
- ♦ Serve warm or chilled.
- ♦ Cointreau can be substituted for rum.

APPLE, WALNUT CALVADOS SAUCE

½ stick butter
1 large apple, peeled, cored and finely chopped

1 cup walnuts
1 cup calvados

- ◆ Melt butter in a sauce pan. Add other ingredients. Simmer for 5 minutes.

MINT SAUCE

1 cup mint, chopped
1 cup vinegar
1 jalapeno, seeded and chopped

1 green onion, chopped
1 Tbls. sugar

- ◆ Combine ingredients in a bowl.

GUACAMOLE

2 large ripe avocados, peeled, pitted and chopped
¼ cup sour cream
2 Tbls. mayonnaise
1 teaspoon cumin

2 green onions, chopped
½ teaspoon salt
2 Tbls. lemon juice
3 cloves garlic, minced
1 teaspoon chili powder

- ◆ Combine all the ingredients in a bowl.

EASY HOLLANDAISE

1 stick butter   Juice of ½ lemon
3 egg yolks

- Melt butter in a small saucepan.
- Into food processor put egg yolks. Blend until smooth.
- Slowly pour butter into processor while blending.
- Add juice of the lemon.
- Serve with broccoli, fish, or on Eggs Benedict.

TOMATO SALSA

2 large ripe tomatoes, finely chopped   ¼ cup cilantro, chopped
Juice of 1 lime   1 teaspoon salt
2 Tbls. olive oil   1 teaspoon fresh ground pepper
2 jalapeno, seeded and finely chopped   2 cloves garlic, minced
                                                 1 green onion, chopped

- Combine all the ingredients in a bowl.

BEARNAISE SAUCE

2 Tbls. white wine vinegar   1 stick butter
2 tablespoons white wine   3 egg yolks
1 tablespoon chopped shallots   ½ lemon
1 tablespoon fresh tarragon   Salt and pepper

- Melt the butter and pour into a food processor. Add egg yolks and lemon juice.
- Combine the vinegar, white wine, shallots and tarragon in a small saucepan. Bring to a boil and reduce to about half.
- Add to food processor mixture. Season with salt and pepper.
- Serve the sauce in a bowl with beef or pork tenderloin.

BREAD AND BUTTER PICKLES

36 small cucumbers, sliced
thinly
¼ cup kosher salt
1 quart cold water
4 cups cider vinegar
4 cups sugar

2 Tbls. mustard seed
1 Tbls. celery seed
1 Tbls. curry powder
2 medium onions, chopped
1 red bell pepper, chopped
1 red pepper, chopped

- ◆ Place the cucumbers in a bowl with the salt and water. Let sit for 3 hours. Drain.
- ◆ Combine all ingredients in a pot. Bring to a boil.
- ◆ Sterilize jars in boiling water. Pour pickles into jars and seal immediately. Store in cool, dark place.

BRANDIED PEACHES

Delicious served over ice cream

2 pounds peaches
2 pounds sugar
1 cup water

1 cinnamon stick, broken
2 teaspoons whole cloves
½ fifth of bourbon or cognac

- ◆ Place the peaches in boiling water and remove peels. Remove pits and cut in half.
- ◆ Bring the sugar and water to a boil. Add peaches, cinnamon and cloves. Simmer until peaches are just tender. Remove peaches.
- ◆ Bring sugar water to boil and simmer until just thickened. Stir in bourbon.
- ◆ Place the peaches in sterilized jars. Pour liquid over peaches.
- ◆ Store in cool, dry place.

RASPBERRY BUTTER

Delicious served with scones or fresh hot rolls

1 stick butter, softened   1 Tbls. lime pr lemon juice
½ pint fresh raspberries

   ♦ Combine the ingredients in a bowl. Make into balls.

SOUR CREAM SAUCE

Serve with pork or on a salad

¼ cup sour cream   1 Tbls. Dijon mustard
¼ cup mayonnaise   2 scallions, chopped

   ♦ Combine ingredients in a bowl.

HORSERADISH SAUCE

2 Tbls. horseradish   1 cup cream, whipped
1 Tbls. Dijon mustard   1 Tbls. lemon juice

   ♦ Fold ingredients together in a bowl.

MAPLE SYRUP DRESSING

Delicious on fruit salads or over mixed greens

¼ cup lemon juice   ¼ cup maple syrup

   ♦ Combine ingredients in a bowl.

HERB CREAM SAUCE

1 stick butter
½ cup flour
1 cup half and half
1 cup cream

4 chives, snipped
¼ cup basil, chopped
2 Tbls. dill, snipped
2 Tbls. parsley, chopped

♦ Melt the butter in a sauce pan. Stir in flour, half and cream until thickened. Add herbs.

SPICY PECANS

1 pound shelled pecans
1 teaspoon cumin
½ cup melted butter

½ teaspoon cayenne
1 Tbls. kosher salt
¼ cup sugar

♦ Preheat oven to 300°
♦ Spread the pecans in a baking dish. Coat pecans with other ingredients.
♦ Bake ½ hour. Do not burn nuts.

CANDIED PECANS

1 pound pecans
1 cup sugar

½ cup corn syrup
½ cup water

♦ Combine the sugar, corn syrup and water in a sauce pan. Heat to 300° on a candy thermometer.
♦ Drop nuts in mixture, a few at a time.
♦ Place nuts on a greased cookie sheet.
♦ Heat syrup if it begins to harden.

DESSERTS

"What calls back the past, like the rich pumpkin pie?"
The Pumpkin
John Greenleaf Whittier

Each year my mother and Barbara de Zalduondo celebrate their birthdays on Nantucket. They have known each other since they were fifteen.

In 1629 apple seeds were planted in Massachusetts by Gov. John Endicott, who had brought the seeds from England. By 1741 New England was exporting apples to the West Indies.

Marshfield, Ma was settled in 1632. During the 19th c the surrounding marshes were drained and cranberries and strawberries cultivated.

The Thimble Islands off Stony Creek, CT were named for the thimble shaped blackberries that used to grow on the islands. Captain Kidd is said to have buried his treasure on Money Island. The Dorchester blackberry received its name in 1841 when an "Improved High Bush Blackberry" was introduced by a gentleman from Dorchester, MA to the Massachusetts Horticultural Society.

Nantucket has delicious blueberries that we have picked since we were children. However, the wild blueberries of Maine have even inspired books that are childhood favorites such as *Blueberries for Sal*. Machias is the wild blueberry capital of Maine. The town was the site of the first naval battle during the Revolution. A two day blueberry festival is held in mid August.

The Baker Chocolate Company was founded in Dorchester, MA in 1764 by John Hannon and Dr. James Baker who leased a mill on the Neponset River and provided Mr. Hannon with the supplies necessary to make the product. By 1778 Hannon's Best Chocolate was being advertised in Boston. However in 1779 Mr. Hannon disappeared at sea after sailing for the West Indies. Dr. Baker took over the company from Mr. Hannon's widow. In 1824 the Hannon Chocolate Company became the Baker Chocolate Company.

Almost one-quarter of the apples grown in Vermont come from around Putney. In 1777 Laomo Baldwin discovered the Baldwin apple in Wilmington, MA. Johnny Appleseed (John Chapman) was born in Leominster, MA. He became famous by spreading his seeds throughout the Ohio Valley, and even had a favorite children's song written about him.

The Stairs pear was first planted in Roxbury, Massachusetts in 1798 by Capt. Thomas Brewer. The Bartlett pear received its name from Enoch Bartlett, who bought the Brewer orchard.

In 1891 Dr. James Naismith nailed peach baskets to the walls of the Springfield, MA YMCA gymnasium, thus inventing the game of basketball.

In 1894 the Whitman Grocery Company of Boston introduced Tapioca Superlative a forerunner of Minute Tapioca. The tapioca is produced from South American manioc and is named for the Minutemen.

Toll House cookies come from an inn near Whitman, MA where Ruth Wakefield made butter cookies with bits of Nestle chocolate bars in the 1930s. Mrs. Wakefield worked with Nestle and in 1939 Nestle packaged the first Nestle Toll House Real Semi-Sweet Chocolate Morsels, otherwise known as chocolate chips.

Ben & Jerry's Ice Cream was founded as an ice cream scoop shop in Burlington, VT in 1978. The factory is now located in Waterbury. Much of this part of Vermont has large dairy farms which supply the company to make more than 180,000 pints of ice cream per week.

Maple Grove Farms of St. Johnsbury, VT was founded in 1915 when Helen Gray and Ethel McClaren used the farm's maple sugar, sweet butter, and butternut trees to make maple candies. They opened a tea room and shipped their candies to every state. The company was bought in 1929 by the Cary Company. Today the company still produces their maple sugar candies, but also salad dressing, and maple syrup.

In 1843 Daniel Forbes while working at Fanueil Market in Boston discovered candied popcorn balls could be made by pouring maple sugar into molds and adding popcorn.

In 1933 Ruth Wakefield began making Toll House cookies in Whitman, MA. She and her husband bought the Tollhouse Inn, built in 1709, in 1930. Nestle Corporation began making chocolate morsels in 1939 and later acquired the rights to the Tollhouse name.

Ben Cohen and Jerry Greenfield opened Ben & Jerry's Ice Cream and Crepes in 1978 in Burlington, VT.

GINGER BLUEBERRY PIE

Pie Crust

1¼ cups flour
1 stick butter, cut into pieces
¼ cup water

3 Tbls. cream cheese

- ♦ Combine the ingredients in a food processor until a ball forms.
- ♦ Roll dough out on a floured board into the shape of the pie plate.

Filling

1 pint blueberries
2 apples, thinly sliced
1 cup cranberries
½ cup brown sugar
4 slices crystallized ginger, chopped

Zest of 1 lemon
1 teaspoon cinnamon
1 teaspoon allspice
1 teaspoon cloves

- ♦ Preheat oven to 400°
- ♦ Combine all ingredients in a bowl.
- ♦ Spoon into the pie crust. Spread topping on mixture
- ♦ Bake pie 45 minutes, or until crust is just browned.

Topping

1 cup old fashioned oats
¼ cup flour

½ cup sugar
½ stick butter, melted

- ♦ Combine the ingredients in a bowl.

FRUIT BOWL

1 pint strawberries
1 pint blueberries
1 pint blackberries

1 pint raspberries
Juice of 1 lime
½ cup dark rum

- ♦ Combine all the ingredients in a bowl. Refrigerate until ready to serve.

RHUBARB GINGER COMPOTE

Serves 4

4 stalks rhubarb, cut into pieces
¾ cup sugar
¼ cup water

2 cups blueberries
4 pieces crystallized ginger, cut into pieces

- ♦ Place the rhubarb, sugar and water in a sauce pan. Bring to a boil.
- ♦ Cook slowly for 5 minutes, or until rhubarb is tender.
- ♦ Remove from heat. Add blueberries and ginger.
- ♦ Cranberries or strawberries can be substituted for blueberries.

STRAWBERRY RHUBARB PIE

Crust – p. 213
1 pint strawberries
2 stalks rhubarb, cut in small pieces
2 eggs, beaten

2 cups heavy cream
1¼ cups sugar
3 Tbls. flour
½ teaspoon nutmeg
2 Tbls. butter

- ♦ Preheat oven to 400°
- ♦ Using 1 pie crust line the pie pan. Place the rhubarb and strawberries in the crust.
- ♦ In a bowl beat the cream. Fold in eggs, sugar, flour, nutmeg and butter.
- ♦ Pour over rhubarb and strawberries.
- ♦ Bake 10 minutes. Reduce heat to 350°. Bake 35 minutes.

FRUIT COMPOTE

Serves 6

3 pears, peeled, pitted and cut in half
1 cup cranberries
3 oranges, peeled and sectioned

6 cloves
2 stick cinnamon
1 cup corn syrup
½ stick butter, melted

- ◆ Preheat oven to 350°
- ◆ Place the pears cut side up in a greased baking dish. Divide the other ingredients among the pears.
- ◆ Bake 20 minutes.

CRANBERRY CHEESECAKE

4 3 oz. packages cream cheese
½ cup sugar
2 eggs
1 Tbls. lemon zest
1 Tbls. lemon juice
½ teaspoon vanilla

2 cups cranberries
½ cup sugar
Zest of 1 orange
1 ginger cookie crust or graham cracker crust

- ◆ Preheat oven to 375°
- ◆ Beat cream cheese. Add sugar, eggs, lemon peel, lemon juice and vanilla.
- ◆ In a food processor combine the cranberries, sugar and zest.
- ◆ Spread cranberry mixture into pie crust. Top with cheese mixture.
- ◆ Bake 35 minutes or until set.
- ◆ Refrigerate until using.
- ◆ Serve garnished with cranberries dipped in sugar.

CRANBERRY SHERBET

1 Tbls. gelatin
½ cup water
4 cups cranberries
2 ½ cups water

2 cups sugar
¼ cup fresh lemon juice
¼ cup fresh orange juice

- ◆ In a bowl sprinkle the ½ cup water over the gelatin to soften.
- ◆ Cook the cranberries in the 2 ½ cups water until the skins pop. Place the cranberries in a food processor.
- ◆ In a sauce pan combine cranberry pulp, sugar, and gelatin. Add the juices. Cook until thickened.
- ◆ Pour into a mold. Freeze at least 4 hours.

CRANBERRY APPLE PIE

1 pie crust – p. 213
2 cups cranberries
2 apples, peeled, seeded and sliced
1 cup pecans
1½ cups sugar
2 eggs

½ cup rolled oats
1 cup flour
1 teaspoon cinnamon
½ teaspoon nutmeg
½ teaspoon ginger
1 stick butter, melted

- ◆ Preheat oven to 325°
- ◆ Spread the cranberries, apples and pecans in pie crust. Sprinkle with ½ the sugar.
- ◆ In a bowl beat together the eggs, flour, oats, spices and butter. Pour into pie crust.
- ◆ Bake 1 hour, until crust is just browned

APPLE CRANBERRY PIE

Crust – p. 213

Filling

3 cups apples, peeled, cored and
thinly sliced
¼ cup walnuts
1 Tbls. grated orange rind
2 Tbls. dark rum
2 cups fresh cranberries
½ stick butter
¼ cup sugar

¼ cup brown sugar
¼ cup flour
½ teaspoon nutmeg
½ teaspoon ground ginger
1 Tbls. cinnamon
¼ teaspoon ground cloves
½ teaspoon ground allspice

- ♦ Preheat oven to 350°.
- ♦ Combine all the ingredients in a bowl, except pie crust.
- ♦ Pour ingredients into pie crust.
- ♦ Bake 45 minutes.
- ♦ 1 cup raisins can be substituted for the cranberries

RUM AND CRANBERRIES OVER ICE CREAM

Serves 4

1 quart vanilla or butter pecan
ice cream
½ cup dark rum

2 cups cranberries
½ cup raisins
½ cup sugar

- ♦ Combine the rum, cranberries, raisins and sugar in a bowl.
- ♦ Spoon the ice cream into bowls. Top with cranberry mixture.

CRANBERRY CAKE

½ stick butter
1 cup sugar
2 cups flour
2 teaspoons baking powder
1 cup milk

2 cups cranberries
1 teaspoon cinnamon
½ teaspoon nutmeg
½ teaspoon cloves

- ♦ Preheat oven to 350°
- ♦ Combine all ingredients in a bowl.
- ♦ Pour into 8x8 inch greased baking dish.
- ♦ Serve with powdered sugar or sauce.

Cranberry Sauce

1 stick butter
1 cup sugar
1 cup cream

1 cup cranberries
Zest of 1 orange

- ♦ Combine all ingredients in a bowl.

CRANBERRY WALNUT PIE

Serves 6-8

Crust – p. 213

Filling

1 stick butter
2 eggs, beaten
½ cup brown sugar
½ cup white sugar

1 teaspoon vanilla
1 teaspoon cinnamon
3 cups fresh cranberries
1 cup walnuts

- ♦ Preheat oven to 325°
- ♦ In a bowl beat the butter, eggs, and sugars. Blend in the other ingredients.
- ♦ Pour into pie shell
- ♦ Bake 1 hour

FOURTH OF JULY MOUSSE

Serves 6

1 envelope unflavored gelatin
2 tablespoons boiling water
Juice of 1 lemon
1 quart strawberries

1 pint blueberries
2 tablespoons rum
½ cup sugar
2 egg yolks
2 cups whipping cream

- ◆ Combine gelatin and water in a small saucepan. Stir in lemon juice.
- ◆ Then add strawberries and blueberries (save 6 for garnish) and rum. Bring to a boil. Cool to room temperature.
- ◆ Beat together egg yolks and sugar in a saucepan, and cook until thickened over low heat. Let cool.
- ◆ Fold the berries into the egg and sugar mixture.
- ◆ Whip the cream until soft peaks are formed and fold into strawberry mixture.
- ◆ Serve individually in wine goblets or glass bowls.
- ◆ Garnish with remaining strawberries.
- ◆ Peaches, raspberries, blackberries or other fruit can be substituted for the strawberries and blueberries.

MAPLE MOUSSE

Serves 6

1 ½ cups maple syrup
2 egg whites, beaten until stiff

Pinch of salt
2 cups heavy cream

- ◆ Cook the maple syrup in a sauce pan until bubbling. Remove from the heat.
- ◆ Add the egg whites stirring constantly. Add salt. Let cool.
- ◆ Whip the cream and fold into the maple syrup mixture.
- ◆ Pour into a mold. Freeze overnight.

RASPBERRY SOUFFLE

Serves 6

2 pints raspberries
1 cup toasted almonds
2 1 ounce packets gelatin
½ cup warm water

4 eggs, separated
½ cup sugar
1 pint whipping cream, whipped

- ♦ Dissolve the gelatin in the water.
- ♦ Beat the egg whites until firm.
- ♦ Fold all the ingredients into a soufflé dish.
- ♦ Chill for at least two hours.

RASPBERRY MOUSSE

Serves 4-6

1 envelope unflavored gelatin
¼ cup water
4 egg yolks, beaten
¾ cup sugar

2 pints raspberries
2 cups heavy cream, beaten
½ cup Grand Marnier

- ♦ Dissolve the gelatin in the water.
- ♦ Combine all ingredients in a soufflé dish.
- ♦ Chill for at least two hours.

PUMPKIN MOUSSE

Serves 6

3 eggs, separated
1 cup sugar
3 cups cooked pumpkin
1 cup heavy cream
½ teaspoon nutmeg
½ teaspoon cinnamon
½ teaspoon ginger

½ teaspoon allspice
½ teaspoon cloves
¼ cup rum
1 Tbls. honey
1 envelope gelatin
¼ cup cold water

- ♦ In a sauce pan beat egg yolks with ½ the sugar. Add the pumpkin, cream and spices. Heat, stirring constantly, until mixture thickens.
- ♦ Sprinkle the gelatin into the water until dissolved. Stir into pumpkin mixture. Remove from heat and chill.
- ♦ Whip the egg whites until stiff. Fold in remaining sugar and pumpkin mixture.
- ♦ Pour into dish and chill.
- ♦ The pumpkin mixture can also be poured into a baked pie crust. Chill and serve with whipped cream.

PUMPKIN COOKIES

1 stick butter
1 ½ cups sugar
1 egg
1 cup pumpkin
1¾ cups flour
2 teaspoons baking powder
½ teaspoon nutmeg

½ teaspoon cloves
½ teaspoon ginger
½ teaspoon cinnamon
½ cup raisins
½ cup pecans

- ♦ Preheat oven to 375°
- ♦ In a bowl cream butter and sugar. Add other ingredients.
- ♦ Drop by spoonfuls onto a cookie sheet.
- ♦ Bake 15 minutes, or until just browned.

PUMPKIN CHEESECAKE

Crust

3 cups ginger, crushed
½ cup sugar

1 cup slivered toasted almonds
or crushed macadamia nuts
½ cup butter, melted

♦ Combine the ingredients and press into 2 pie plates.

Filling

16 ounces cream cheese
1 cup light cream
1 cup pumpkin
½ cup sugar
¼ cup maple syrup
2 Tbls. brandy
4 egg yolks

4 egg whites, beaten until stiff
3 tablespoons flour
1 teaspoon vanilla
1 teaspoon cinnamon
½ teaspoon ginger
½ teaspoon nutmeg
¼ teaspoon salt

♦ Combine all ingredients except egg whites. Fold in egg whites.
♦ Pour filling into 2 crusts. Bake 325° for one hour.

PUMPKIN BREAD PUDDING

Serves 6

½ cup sugar
2 cups heavy cream
3 eggs
2 cups pumpkin
1 teaspoon cinnamon
2 Tbls. fresh grated ginger

½ teaspoon nutmeg
½ teaspoon allspice
¼ teaspoon cloves
6 cups French bread, cubed
1 cup pecans

♦ Preheat oven to 350°
♦ In a sauce pan heat the sugar, cream and eggs. Add pumpkin and spices.
♦ Arrange the bread and pecans in a greased baking dish. Pour the egg mixture on top.
♦ Bake 30-35 minutes or until custard is set.
♦ Serve with Crème Anglaise or whipped cream.

CHOCOLATE BREAD PUDDING

Serves 6

6 cups French bread, cubed
2 ½ cups half and half
8 oz. chocolate
1 teaspoon vanilla
1½ sticks butter
8 eggs, beaten

½ cup dark rum
1 teaspoon cinnamon
1 cup slivered toasted almonds
½ cup coconut

- ◆ Preheat oven to 350°
- ◆ Heat half and half, chocolate, vanilla and butter in a sauce pan till boiling. Reduce heat and simmer for 5 minutes. Remove from heat. Cool. Add eggs, rum and cinnamon.
- ◆ Layer bread, almonds and coconut in greased baking dish. Pour sauce over top.
- ◆ Bake 30-35 minutes or until custard is set
- ◆ Garnish with strawberries, fresh mint and whipped cream or ice cream.

GINGER BREAD PUDDING

Serves 6

½ cup sugar
2 cups heavy cream
3 eggs
6 cups French bread, cubed

½ cup crystallized ginger, chopped
1 cup raisins
1 cup candied fruit

- ◆ Preheat oven to 350°
- ◆ In a sauce pan heat the sugar, cream and eggs.
- ◆ Arrange the bread and rest of ingredients in a greased baking dish. Pour the egg mixture on top.
- ◆ Bake 30-35 minutes or until custard is set.
- ◆ Serve with Crème Anglaise or whipped cream.

LEMON BLUEBERRY CAKE

1 stick butter, softened
½ cups sugar
1 ½ cups flour
1 teaspoon baking powder
1 cup sour cream

¼ cup lemon juice
Zest of 1 lemon
1 pint blueberries
¼ cup poppy seeds

- ♦ Preheat oven to 350°
- ♦ Cream the butter and sugar. Add other ingredients.
- ♦ Pour into greased 9 x 13 baking dish or 2 cake pans. Bake 45 minutes, or until toothpick comes out clean.
- ♦ Dust with powdered sugar.

PEACH UPSIDE-DOWN CAKE

Batter

½ stick butter
1 cup sugar
2 eggs
1 cup sour cream

1½ teaspoons baking powder
1½ cups flour
1 teaspoon vanilla

- ♦ In a bowl beat the butter, sugar, eggs, sour cream, baking powder, flour and vanilla.

½ stick butter
½ cup brown sugar, packed
4 large peaches, peeled, pitted and sliced

Juice of ½ lemon
1 cup pecans or walnuts

- ♦ Preheat oven to 350°.
- ♦ In a 9" x 13" glass baking dish melt the butter in the oven. remove and sprinkle the brown sugar evenly over the butter.
- ♦ Arrange the peach slices on top of the brown sugar. Sprinkle with the lemon juice and pecans.
- ♦ Pour batter over the peaches.
- ♦ Bake 40 minutes or until a toothpick comes out clean.
- ♦ Remove and immediately turn upside down on a serving platter. Leave pan over the cake for a few minutes before removing.
- ♦ Serve plain, or with ice cream.

BOSTON CREAM PIE

Growing up we loved desserts. This was a favorite.

1 stick butter
2 eggs
2 teaspoons baking powder
1¼ cups sugar

1 ½ cups flour
¼ teaspoon salt
½ cup cream
1 teaspoon vanilla

- Preheat oven to 350°
- Grease 2 cake pans and sprinkle with a small amount of flour.
- In a bowl cream the butter and sugar. Beat in eggs and other ingredients.
- Divide batter between two cake pans.
- Bake 35 minutes, or until toothpick comes out clean. Cool and remove from pans.
- Place one layer of the cake upside down. Spread with custard.
- Place other cake layer on top. Spread with chocolate frosting.

Custard

½ cup cream
½ cup milk
½ cup sugar

4 teaspoons cornstarch
2 eggs, beaten
1 teaspoon vanilla

- In a sauce pan heat cream, milk and sugar. Remove from heat and stir in cornstarch until thickened. Stir in eggs and vanilla. Cool in refrigerator.

Chocolate Frosting

4 oz. semi-sweet chocolate
2 Tbls. butter
½ cup cream

½ cup confectioners' sugar
½ teaspoon vanilla

- Heat the butter and chocolate in a sauce pan. Remove from heat. Stir in cream and sugar until thickened. Add vanilla.

POACHED PEARS

Serves 12

12 large ripe pears
Juice of 2 lemons
2 cups sugar

2 whole cloves
1 stick cinnamon

- Peel the pears, cut in half and remove the seeds.
- In a large pan place all the ingredients and boil until the pears are soft.
- Serve on a platter with cut sides up.
- Whipped cream or ice cream can be served with pears.

POACHED PEARS II

Serves 6

1 bottle red wine
½ cup sugar
2 cinnamon sticks
6 whole cloves

1 lemon, thinly sliced
1 orange, thinly sliced
6 firm pears, peeled, cored and
cut in half lengthwise

- Cook in a sauce pan for ½ hour until pears are tender.
- Serve in bowls with ice cream or whipped cream.

STIR FRY APPLES

Serves 6

½ stick butter
6 medium apples, cored and
sliced
½ cup maple syrup
1 cup walnuts

1 teaspoon cinnamon
½ teaspoon nutmeg
½ teaspoon ginger
½ allspice

- Melt butter in skillet. Add apples. Cook for 5 minutes, until just tender. Stir in other ingredients.
- Serve with whipped cream or ice cream.

BAKED APPLES

Serves 6

6 medium apples, cored
1 cup cranberries
½ cup maple syrup
1 teaspoon cinnamon

½ teaspoon ginger
¼ teaspoon nutmeg
1 cup walnuts

- ◆ Preheat oven to 350°
- ◆ Combine all the ingredients, except apples in a bowl.
- ◆ Stuff the apples with the mixture.
- ◆ Place in greased baking dish.
- ◆ Bake ½ hour.

BAKED APPLES II

Serves 6

6 large cooking apples, cored
1 cup pecans
½ stick butter, melted
½ cup honey

½ cup dried apricots
½ cup dried cranberries
¼ cup dark rum
Whipped cream or ice cream

- ◆ Preheat the oven to 400°.
- ◆ Remove the cores from the apples.
- ◆ In a bowl combine the pecans, butter, honey, apricots, cranberries and rum.
- ◆ Grease a baking dish and place the apples in the dish. Divide up the pecan mixture and place in the apples.
- ◆ Bake the apples for 45 minutes.
- ◆ Serve with whipped cream or ice cream

APPLE CRISP

Serves 6

6 medium apples, cored and sliced	Juice of 1 lemon 1 cup cranberries

- Preheat oven to 350°
- Combine the ingredients in a baking dish.
- Sprinkle topping on apples.
- Bake ½ hour.
- Serve with whipped cream or ice cream.

Topping

½ cup old fashioned oats	1 teaspoon cinnamon
¼ cup flour	½ teaspoon ginger
1 stick butter melted	1 cup walnuts

- Combine ingredients in a bowl.

APPLESAUCE

Serves 6

6 large apples, peeled, cored and quartered	½ teaspoon ginger
½ cup water	¼ teaspoon nutmeg
¾ cup sugar	½ teaspoon allspice
1 teaspoon cinnamon	¼ teaspoon cloves

- Combine ingredients in sauce pan. Cook until apples are tender.

APPLE GINGERBREAD

½ stick butter
½ cup brown sugar
1 teaspoon cinnamon

2 apples, peeled, cored and sliced
1 cup cranberries
½ cup walnuts

- Preheat oven to 350°
- Melt butter in square baking dish
- In a bowl combine sugar, cinnamon, apples, and cranberries. Add to butter
- Pour gingerbread on top.
- Bake 35-40 minutes, or toothpick comes out clean.
- Serve with whipped cream or ice cream

Gingerbread

1 stick butter
½ cup sugar
1 egg
½ cup dark molasses
1 ½ cups flour
½ teaspoon salt

1 teaspoon baking powder
1 Tbls. ginger
½ teaspoon cloves
½ teaspoon nutmeg
½ teaspoon cinnamon
½ cup boiling water

- Combine the ingredients in a bowl.

APPLE PUDDING

Serves 6

2 apples, peeled, cored
½ stick butter, melted
3 cups French bread, cubed
½ cup sugar
2 cups half and half

Zest of 1 lemon
3 eggs
1 teaspoon vanilla
¼ teaspoon nutmeg

- Preheat oven to 350°
- In a sauce pan heat the sugar, half and half, lemon zest, vanilla and nutmeg.
- Arrange the apples and bread in a baking dish. Pour butter on top and egg mixture. Bake 45 minutes, or until set.

APPLE CRANBERRY CAKE

1 stick butter
1 cup sugar
2 cups flour
1 teaspoon cinnamon
½ teaspoon ginger
½ teaspoon allspice
¼ teaspoon nutmeg
1 ½ teaspoons baking powder

2 eggs
1 teaspoon vanilla
4 apples, peeled, cored and chopped
1 cup cranberries
1 cup walnuts

- ♦ Preheat oven to 350°
- ♦ Cream butter and sugar. Stir in other ingredients.
- ♦ Pour batter into greased 13x9 baking dish or two cake pans.
- ♦ Bake for 50 minutes or until toothpick comes out clean.
- ♦ Frost with cream cheese frosting.

Cream Cheese Frosting

½ stick butter
1 3 oz. package cream cheese
1 teaspoon vanilla

2 cups powdered sugar

- ♦ Cream ingredients in a bowl.

SWEET POTATO PIE

Pie crust – p. 213, add 1 cup chopped pecans
4 eggs
½ cup heavy cream
½ cup orange juice
2 cups sweet potatoes, cooked and mashed
½ cup sugar

2 Tbls. honey
1 teaspoon vanilla
½ teaspoon nutmeg
½ teaspoon cinnamon
½ teaspoon ginger
½ teaspoon cloves
½ cup pecans

- ♦ Preheat oven to 350º
- ♦ In a bowl beat the eggs and cream. Add the rest of the ingredients. Pour into the pie shell. Bake 40 minutes or until set.
- ♦ Serve with whipped cream, ice cream or just plain.

BLUEBERRY PIE

2 crusts – p. 213

Filling

2 pints blueberries
1 cup sugar
3 Tbls. flour
½ teaspoon cinnamon
¼ teaspoon nutmeg

¼ teaspoon cloves
2 Tbls. lemon juice
2 Tbls. butter, melted
1 Tbls. lemon zest

- ◆ Preheat oven to 400°
- ◆ In a bowl combine the ingredients. Spoon into 1 pie crust.
- ◆ Cut the other pie crust into 1 inch wide strips. Lay as lattice on pie.
- ◆ Bake 35-40 minutes, until crust is just browned.

PEAR AND WALNUT PIE

2 pie crusts – p. 213

2 large pears, peeled, cored and sliced
½ cup sugar
2 Tbls. flour
Zest of 1 lemon
¼ cup raisins

½ cup walnuts
1 teaspoon cinnamon
Juice of 1 lemon
2 teaspoons water
2 Tbls. dark rum

- ◆ Preheat the oven to 350°.
- ◆ Place one of the pie crusts in a pie pan. Roll out the other pie crust and cut into slices to make a lattice top.
- ◆ In a bowl combine all the ingredients.
- ◆ Pour into the pie crust. Top with lattice.
- ◆ Bake 40 minutes or until just browned.
- ◆ Serve with ice cream or whipped cream.

PEANUT BUTTER PIE

Crust

24 chocolate vanilla wafer cookies, crushed

½ stick butter, melted
1 cup peanuts, crushed

♦ Combine the cookies, peanuts and butter in a pie plate. Pat into plate.

Filling

1 package cream cheese
1 cup peanut butter
½ cup sugar
1 teaspoon vanilla

1 cup heavy cream
1 square semisweet chocolate, shaved

♦ In a bowl combine all the ingredients except chocolate. Pour into the pie plate. Refrigerate at least 4 hours.
♦ Garnish with chocolate shavings.

VANILLA CUSTARD WITH FRESH BERRIES

Serves 4

4 egg yolks
½ cup sugar
½ cup Chardonnay

1 Tbls. kirsh or rum
2 pints raspberries, strawberries, blueberries or blackberries.

♦ Combine the eggs and sugar in a sauce pan, beating until mixture thickens. Slowly stir in wine and kirsch. Do not boil.
♦ Divide the berries between 4 martini or parfait glasses. Serve with custard.

WHITE CHOCOLATE CAKE

½ cup milk
½ stick butter
6 egg yolks
1 cup sugar
½ teaspoon vanilla

1 cup flour
1 teaspoon baking powder
½ pound white chocolate, cut into small pieces

- ♦ Heat milk and butter in a sauce pan until butter melts.
- ♦ In a bowl beat egg yolks until creamy. Add sugar and vanilla. Stir in flour and baking powder. Gently pour milk into bowl. Add ¼ pound chocolate.
- ♦ Pour into greased 9 x 9 baking pan. Bake 30-35 minutes, or until just browned. Remove from baking dish and cut in half. Place one half cake, cut side up on a plate.
- ♦ Spread cream filling on bottom layer. Place other layer on top.
- ♦ Drizzle glaze over top of cake.
- ♦ Grate the remaining white chocolate and sprinkle on top of glaze.
- ♦ Chocolate can also be melted and drizzled over glaze.

Apricot Glaze

1½ cups apricot jam
¼ cup sugar

¼ cup water
3 Tbl.s kirsch

- ♦ Heat the ingredients in a sauce pan.

Butter Cream Filling

½ stick butter
4 oz. white chocolate, cut in slivers

1 cup powdered sugar
2 Tbls. cream
½ teaspoon vanilla

- ♦ Combine ingredients in a bowl until smooth.

233

RICE PUDDING

Rice Pudding is an old New England recipe. Six recipes for this were included in the first American cookbook written by Amelia Simmons. One recipe included rice, cinnamon, milk, nutmeg, rose-water, eggs, and puff paste.

Serves 6

½ cup uncooked rice
3 cups milk
1 teaspoon orange zest
1 teaspoon lemon zest
2 Tbls. butter
3 eggs
½ cup sugar

½ cup sugar
1 teaspoon vanilla
½ cup candied fruit
2 Tbls. rum
½ cup slivered almonds
1 cup cream
½ teaspoon nutmeg

- ◆ Bring the milk and rice to a boil in a sauce pan. Add orange and lemon zest. Simmer 15 minutes or until rice is tender. Add butter.
- ◆ Beat eggs in a bowl. Add sugar and vanilla. Pour slowly into rice mixture. Put in refrigerator and chill for at least two hours.
- ◆ Combine the fruit, rum and nuts in a bowl. Stir into rice mixture.
- ◆ Beat the cream until peaks form. Fold into rice mixture.
- ◆ Divide mixture between 6 bowls or parfait glasses. Sprinkle nutmeg on each serving.

BROWNIES

1 stick butter
2 oz. unsweetened chocolate
¼ cup cocoa
1 cup sugar
1 package chocolate chips

½ cup dark rum
1¼ cups flour
1 teaspoon baking powder
2 eggs
1 cup pecans

- ◆ Preheat oven to 350°.
- ◆ Melt butter, chocolate and cocoa in a sauce pan. Remove from heat and stir in remaining ingredients. Pour into a greased baking dish.
- ◆ Bake 45 minutes or until toothpick comes out clean.

WHITE CHOCOLATE MOUSSE WITH BLUEBERRY SAUCE

Serves 6

8 oz. white chocolate
1 envelope gelatin
¼ cup water

2 cups heavy cream
¾ cup sugar
2 Tbls. rum or kirsch

- ♦ Melt the chocolate in a sauce pan.
- ♦ Dissolve the gelatin in the water.
- ♦ Beat cream until peaks form. Fold in sugar, gelatin and chocolate.
- ♦ Pour into a soufflé dish and chill.
- ♦ Serve with a bowl of the blueberry sauce and white chocolate shavings.

Blueberry Sauce

2 pints blueberries
¼ cup sugar

¼ cup rum or kirsch

- ♦ Place ingredients in food processor until smooth.

CHOCOLATE PEANUT COOKIES

Makes about 18 cookies

1 stick butter
½ cup sugar
½ cup brown sugar
1¼ cups flour

1 teaspoon baking powder
1 cup chocolate chips
1 egg
1 cup peanut butter

- ♦ Preheat oven to 375°.
- ♦ In a bowl cream the sugars and butter. Add the eggs. Beat in the flour, baking, powder and chocolate chips.
- ♦ Drop batter by large spoonfuls onto a cookie sheet. Make indentation in each and put in a spoonful of peanut butter.
- ♦ Bake 10-12 minutes or until just browned and crisp.

OATMEAL LACE COOKIES

1 cup flour
½ teaspoon salt
½ teaspoon baking powder
1 cup sugar
1 cup old fashioned oats

¼ cup cream
¼ cup light corn syrup
1 stick butter, melted
1 teaspoon vanilla

- ♦ Preheat oven to 375°
- ♦ In a bowl combine all the ingredients until well blended.
- ♦ Drop by teaspoons onto an ungreased cookie sheet, 4 inches apart.
- ♦ Bake for 6-8 minutes or until just browned.
- ♦ Let stand a minute or two before removing from cookie sheet.
- ♦ Serve with ice cream.

OATMEAL CHOCOLATE CHIP COOKIES

Makes about 20 cookies

½ cup brown sugar
½ cup white sugar
1 stick butter
1 egg
1½ cups old- fashioned oats

1 cup flour
1 teaspoon vanilla
1 package chocolate chips
1 cup walnuts or pecans

- ♦ Preheat oven to 375°.
- ♦ Cream butter and sugars. Add other ingredients.
- ♦ Drop by large spoonful on an ungreased cookie sheet.
- ♦ Bake 10-15 minutes or until just browned.

CHOCOLATE CHIP COOKIES

2 sticks butter
1 cup sugar
1 cup brown sugar
1 teaspoon vanilla
2 eggs

2 ½ cups flour
1 teaspoon baking powder
1 package chocolate chips
½ cup pecans
½ cup dried cranberries

- Preheat oven to 375°
- Cream the butter and sugars in a bowl. Beat in vanilla, eggs, flour and baking powder.
- Fold in chips, pecans and cranberries.
- Drop by spoonfuls onto an ungreased cookie sheet.
- Bake 10-12 minutes, or until just browned.

CRANBERRY BUNS

2 Tbls. dark rum
½ cup cranberries
½ cup currants or raisins
2 cups flour
½ cup brown sugar
½ stick butter

¼ cup milk
1 egg
1 teaspoon baking powder
½ teaspoon nutmeg
½ teaspoon cinnamon
¼ cup coconut

- Preheat oven to 375°
- In a bowl combine the rum, cranberries and currants.
- In another bowl combine the rest of the ingredients.
- Stir in the cranberry mixture.
- Drop by spoonfuls onto cookie sheet.
- Bake 12-15 minutes, or until just browned.
- Remove and cool on rack.

COCONUT SQUARES

2 sticks butter, melted
1½ cups graham cracker crumbs
½ package chocolate bits

½ package butterscotch bits
1 cup pecans or walnuts
3 ½ ounces coconut
1 can condensed sweetened milk

- Preheat oven to 375°.
- In a 9 x 13 pan pour in the melted butter and top with the graham cracker crumbs.
- Top with chocolate bits, nuts, and coconut. Pour the condensed milk over everything.
- Bake for about 25 minutes or until golden.

RICE KRISPY TREATS

6 cups Rice Krispies
10 oz. package marshmallows

½ stick butter

- Melt the butter and add marshmallows until completely melted. Stir in Rice Krispies.
- Press into an 8" square pan lined with wax paper. Do not bake.
- Cut into squares.

PEANUT BRITTLE

1½ cups sugar
¾ cups light corn syrup
3 Tbls.water
1 teaspoon vanilla extract

3 Tbls. butter
1 teaspoon baking soda
1½ cups salted peanuts

- In a large pot combine the sugar, corn syrup, water and vanilla. Stir until mixture boils. Cook until a candy thermometer registers 280°. Remove from heat.
- Add butter and stir until the butter is melted. Return to heat and candy thermometer registers 300°. Remove from heat and add baking soda. Stir in peanuts.
- Pour into a buttered cookie sheet. Let cool. Break into small pieces.

INDEX

248

ABOUT THE AUTHOR

Katie Barney Moose, born in Baltimore, is a descendant of old New England whaling families and the Clagett (Claggett) family of Maryland. She has lived in many of the U.S.' great culinary, architectural, historical and waterside gems- New Castle, DE; Newport and Providence, RI; Cold Spring Harbor, NY; San Francisco; Philadelphia; Greenwich, CT; Alexandria, VA; Washington, DC; and New York City. She presently resides in Annapolis, Maryland;

Mrs. Moose is in the process of publishing a series of regional cookbooks, and guidebooks on the different regions of the Chesapeake Bay and cookbooks on New England. She has also published "Uniquely Delaware" and "Uniquely Rhode Island" for Heinemann Publishers of New York. She was the co-author of "The Best of Newport, the Newport Guidebook", several publications on the fiber optic telecommunications business, and is a consultant on international business and protocol. Her hobbies beside gourmet cooking and fine wine, include history, sailing, genealogy, theology and travel.

ORDER FORM FOR CONDUIT PRESS BOOKS

Please send me _____copies of New England's Bounty @ $18.95

Please send me _____copies of Chesapeake's Bounty II @ $17.95

Please send me _____copies of Maryland's Western Shore: The Guidebook @ $15.95

Please send me _____copies of Annapolis: The Guidebook @ $13.95

Please send me _____copies of Eastern Shore of Maryland: The Guidebook @ $15.95

Add postage for 1st book @ $4.00 _____
Postage for each additional book @ $1.00 _____
Gift wrap per book @ $2.00 _____
Total order _____

❑ Check or money order enclosed
❑ Make payable to Conduit Press

Mail to: Conduit Press
111 Conduit Street
Annapolis, MD 21401

Ship books to:

Name_____

Address_____

_____

Telephone_____

For further information please
• Call 410-280-5272
• Fax 410-263-5380
• E-mail: kamoose@erols.com